"Anne Neuberger has found a wonderful way to celebrate the millennium with our children. By examining our heroes through the centuries she has put the Christian Millenniums under a microscope for all to see. This project is too big for the refrigerator. Dedicate a wall and plenty of time to walk with your child into their own century where they are the heroes and the saints."

Father John Swing
Pastor, Sacred Heart, Nekoosa
St. Alexanders, Port Edwards, WI

"For several years I have been looking for a good book written about the lives of saints to use with our students. Thanks to author Anne Neuberger we now have an excellent resource for both librarians and classroom teachers. Neuberger has put together a diverse collection of saints' stories from the past 20 centuries, each offering a historical glimpse of what was happening throughout the world during their lifetime. Also included are well planned activities which will help students relate their lives to the lives of saints. Neuberger concludes each chapter with ideas on creating a timeline with the students and a list of more saints of that century. I highly recommend this book!"

Saundra Knauff
School Librarian, Christ the King–St. Thomas the Apostle School
Chair, St. Paul-Minneapolis Archdiocesan Librarians' Committee

"The subitle *Mystics and Martyrs, Healers and Hermits, Soldiers and Seekers* indicates the great diversity of the saints who were a blessing to the church and the world in their own time and for all time. Anne Neuberger takes 'the communion of saints' to a new level of awareness for the whole people of God. As adults and children go through these stories, one wonders who God will call forth to serve as witnesses in word and deed in the days and years ahead? By reflecting on the lives of the saints presented here, adults and children alike are invited to identify the gifts God has bestowed upon them to be used in response to the very real challenges of the 21st century."

Ralph Baumgartner
Assistant to the Bishop, Saint Paul Area Synod
Evangelical Lutheran Church in America

"Who says church history is dull? Anne Neuberger has found a formula for keeping our rich religious heritage alive for all ages. *Stories of Saints through the Centuries* is a treasure chest of vivid historical sketches, sparkling narrative, fresh dramatic readings, and 'can't wait' activities for the classroom or home.

"Parents, teachers, and catechists will enjoy these adventures as much as the children they guide."

Leo Jacoby
Deanery Coordinator, Stevens Point, WI
Diocese of LaCrosse

"Anne Neuberger's book is a teacher's delight! A distinctive array of saints come alive on the pages against the backdrop of centuries of church history. Varied activities conclude each story and help children glean wisdom for their own lives. These saints are heroic role models who continue to walk with us as companions on our journey."

Sr. Carole MacKenthun, RSM
St. Catherine School, Spring Lake, NJ
Author of *Saints Alive* series

"So many Catholic parents wonder how best to communicate the richness of our religious heritage and the meaning of our faith to children today. Anne Neuberger helps us to accomplish this task. She brings a saint-a-century from our shared story, placing the saints in their historical and social contexts. *Stories of Saints through the Centuries* also helps us take advantage of storytelling techniques that capture children's attention."

Kris Berggren
Writer and mother of three
National Catholic Reporter columnist

"This is a valuable resource for the elementary educator. Through the lenses of world history, geography and church history, Anne guides readers to a creative perspective on the church and its saints. She suggests activities and readings to further involve the students in seeing saints as part of their heritage and their present world."

Jane Hilger
Catholic Education and Formation Ministries
Social Mission Coordinator
St. Paul, MN

"Anne Neuberger's *Stories of Saints through the Centuries* is an exciting way to learn about our church's saints and also to enter into the the history of our church. Keeping a time line helps visualize the many changes our church has seen. This treasury of hands-on creative activities, choral readings, stories, and skits will help children enter into the history of the church as we celebrate the lives of its saints.

Elizabeth Arend
Director of Religious Education
St. John Vianney Church
South St. Paul, MN

"Anne Neuberger's new book on the saints is an answer to the prayers of parents and catechists searching for help in passing on the stories and traditions of their Catholic faith. Saul, for example, tells a first-person version of his transformation into Paul the Evangelist. Margaret Bosco asks, 'Have you heard about my son Father John Bosco?' The saga of new American saint Elizabeth Seton has seven parts for oral reading. Neuberger's story of St. John Kanty, the Polish hero, lends itself to a puppet show.

"Best of all, Neuberger sets the stage with each story by placing the saints in the global historical perspective of their times. What a great way to combine building up Catholic identity, world history, and faith formation."

Bob Zyskowski
The Catholic Spirit
St. Paul, MN

Mystics & Martyrs, Healers & Hermits, Soldiers & Seekers...

Stories of Saints through the Centuries

Anne E. Neuberger

TWENTY-THIRD PUBLICATIONS

Mystic, CT 06355

Dedication

To my Elizabeth Hyerim
who arrived on the feast of Saint Elizabeth
and to the memory of Uncle Peter Altmann
who gave me my first book of saints.

Acknowledgments

Paul and Lucia Marincel, Loretta Neuberger, Jeannie Podvin, Sandy Knauff, Mary Ellen Rieland, and Mary Carol Kendzia.

Twenty-Third Publications
185 Willow Street
P.O. Box 180
Mystic, CT 06355
(860) 536-2611
(800) 321-0411

ISBN: 0-89622-984-X
Library of Congress Catalog Card Number: 99-71170
Printed in the U.S.A.

Table of Contents

Introduction

Can you believe we have twenty centuries of Christianity behind us? In this vast expanse of time, Christianity has been lived out in ways as numerous and distinct as historical circumstances and individual personalities allow. Granted, there have been many deeds done in the name of Christ that have been anything but Christian. Still, the essence of what Jesus taught and what is asked of his followers still shines in the world, two thousand years after his death and resurrection.

At this time of closure on the twentieth century, as we emerge into a new millennium, it is good to ask about the people who have kept the light of Christ alive. This knowledge gives us hope and guidance for the future. It celebrates our rich heritage, and gives us an opportunity to pass on this heritage to our children. Among the torch bearers of our past, of course, are the saints.

Catholic children are blessed with a legacy of saint stories that can counsel, delight, challenge, and comfort. Offering them a great variety of these stories gives them many models to ponder, and provides direction as they struggle to live out their own callings.

We believe in the communion of saints. This tells us that Christ's Church is made up of all of us—those of us who have already lived and died, and those of us who are currently living. As we look back on thousands of years of civilization, we can also look back on two thousand years of Church history, with its many tales of persons united with us in the communion of saints.

This book attempts to give children some of their rich saint story heritage within the history of the past twenty centuries. By placing the stories of the saints in the context of the times in which they lived, these stories will also give children a sense of the history of their Church and of civilization.

In the following chapters, you will find stories of a saint or two for each of the twenty centuries since Christ's resurrection. These people loved Jesus and found ways to live out that love. They teach us that no matter how gifted or limited by life we are, we can do as Jesus teaches.

Anthony of Egypt, in the third century, was called to live a quiet, contemplative life in the desert. Sixteen hundred years later, John Bosco led a boisterous life in the city, educating and sheltering hundreds of boys, and contending with political strife to do so. We find saints who lived in times of peace. Their faith and efforts taught others about God's love and compassion.

There are saints who struggled through times of war. Some ministered to others during plagues or famine. Some saints withdrew from the hubbub of life, quietly touching others through prayer and example. Others lived in the thick of things, and still others straddled both of these worlds. Some were wealthy, some lowly. All were challenged by the times in which they lived.

Each chapter is composed of three main sections:

The times. In the opening section, significant events of each century are given along with a glimpse of life in many different parts of the world. This section is addressed to teachers and parents who can share this information with children in whatever way fits their circumstances. It can open opportunities for discussion. Some topics could be: were the motives behind a leader's actions good or bad? Does the end always justify the means? Are wars necessary? Is our time more or less "civilized" than another?

The story. Each century hosted many saints. One or more are presented here in a story which can be read by the children, by an adult, or both. The stories are presented in a number of different styles, all of which involve young listeners.

The activities. Most saints lived in eras different from ours. Nonetheless, each saint offers us a message for our own time. With each story are additional activities that reflect the saint's life, message, or time, helping children connect the saint's example to their own lives.

We need everyone's talents and energies as we proceed forward together in our lives and in our faith. May these saint stories encourage children to ask: "What are my gifts, and how am I being called to use them?"

Creating a timeline

To help readers understand how Christianity has evolved, as well as to better understand the lives of the saints during the times in which they lived, create a visual aid with a timeline. Use the examples of the timelines on the next two pages, as well as the information from the opening section of each chapter, to make your timeline. You can make a long timeline, adding information about each new century as you go through it with your class or at home. Or have the children make individual timelines on 8 1/2 inch by 11 inch sheets of paper. These can then be displayed separately or taped together to form a long, connected timeline.

In each chapter there is a closing section that lists names and dates of other great Christians who lived in each century. Their names can be placed on the timeline, and their stories can be researched and enjoyed, too.

By looking at the saints in the context of a timeline, young readers may see that there has been continuous progress throughout history. Christians have made great strides in living their faith despite problems such as greed, war, illness, and hatred. In seeing the wide variety of personalities and talents of the saints, children may better understand Saint Paul's words: "There are many different gifts, but it is always the same Spirit. There are many different ways of serving, but it is always the same Lord. There are many different forms of activity, but in everyone it is the same God who is at work in them all" (1 Cor 12:4–6).

Use this example if you are making a vertical timeline, with one page for each of the twenty centuries in this book.

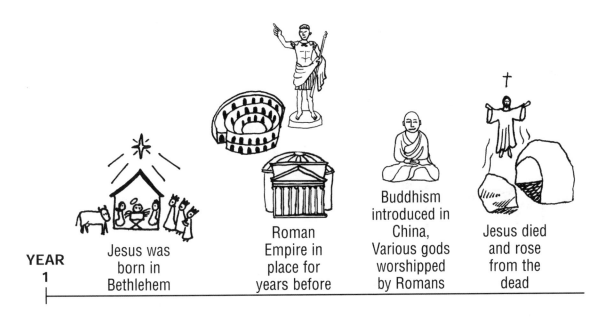

YEAR 1

Jesus was born in Bethlehem

Roman Empire in place for years before

Buddhism introduced in China, Various gods worshipped by Romans

Jesus died and rose from the dead

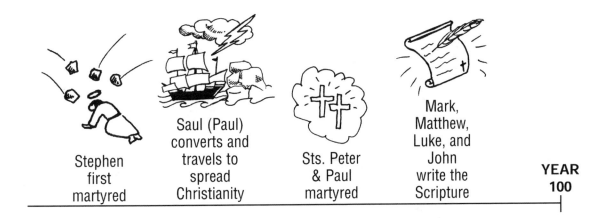

Stephen first martyred

Saul (Paul) converts and travels to spread Christianity

Sts. Peter & Paul martyred

Mark, Matthew, Luke, and John write the Scripture

YEAR 100

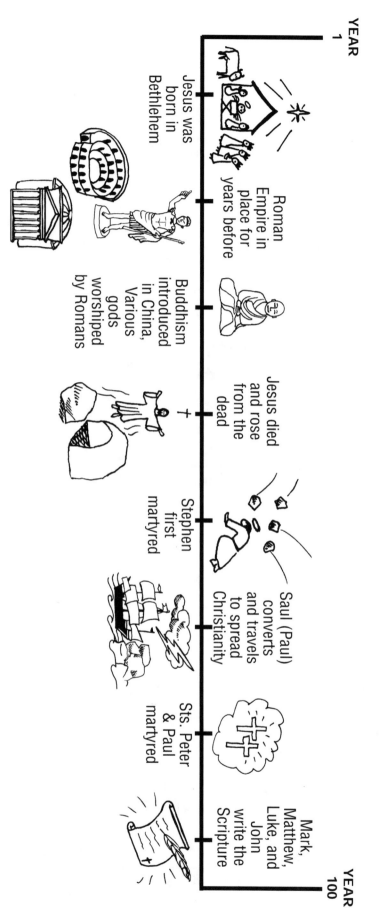

U se this example if you are making a long, horizontal timeline connecting all or part of the twenty centuries in this book.

YEAR 1

Jesus was born in Bethlehem

Roman Empire in place for years before

Buddhism introduced in China, Various gods worshiped by Romans

Jesus died and rose from the dead

Stephen first martyred

Saul (Paul) converts and travels to spread Christianity

Sts. Peter & Paul martyred

Mark, Matthew, Luke, and John write the Scripture

YEAR 100

Paul of Tarsus

Died c. 67 AD

The "first century," as we in the Western world refer to it, was not the beginning of the world, nor even the beginning of recorded history. For many thousands of years, people lived and loved and laughed all over the world before this so-called first century.

We Christians, however, measure time from when Jesus was born. We recognize the many years, important people, and events that came before him, but because Jesus's life on earth is so important to our faith, we use that piece of history as a reference point to count our days. When we say "the first century," we are referring to the year in which Jesus was born, and to the one hundred years following that.

In this first century, then, Jesus was born in Bethlehem, grew up in Nazareth, died and rose from the dead in Jerusalem. The world was a busy and amazing place then. Many years before, the republic of Rome had expanded through warfare to become a great empire. During Jesus' time, it included Spain, Gaul, most of northern Africa and Egypt, the south-ern Balkans, Greece, Syria, and England. The Romans built towns and cities and networks of roads to connect them. They introduced better ways of farming and sophisticated water systems. Some examples of their great architecture still stand today, like the Colosseum in Rome, built in the year 80, which could hold 50,000 spectators.

Wealthy persons owned villas, which consisted of great houses and fields of rich farm land. The lord and his family lived in homes built of stone or brick, along with a bailiff (who was the overseer of the estate) and slaves to work the farm. Travel for the privileged was done in a *carpentum*, a heavy, two-wheeled carriage that looked not unlike the covered wagons that would cross North America centuries later.

Civilization was progressing elsewhere, too. In China, the Han dynasty was in power, using a sophisticated form of government for its own vast empire. Technology had produced a breastplate harness, making it easier for horses to pull heavy loads. Bamboo bridges spanned some of the gorges in the Himalayan Mountains, acupuncture was in use, and papermaking was invented at this time.

Buddhism was introduced in China during this century, and a variety of religions were practiced throughout the Roman empire. Official Roman gods changed with the changing of emperors, while local cults flourished here and there. Greek philosophy influenced much thinking, and large communities of Jews populated the empire.

Also in this first century, a new religion sprang up, first among some of the Jewish people, then also among non-Jews, called Gentiles. This religion would some day be called Christianity, and it would play a major role in the centuries to come. Its roots, of course, would always be traced to the birth of the child Jesus to poor parents in a stable in Bethlehem.

Around this same time (10 AD), another Jewish boy was born. His name was Saul, and he was born to wealth and comfort in the Greek-Roman city of Tarsus, on the southern coast of Asia Minor (now Turkey). He and Jesus never met while both lived on earth. Yet Saul turned out to be one of the most influential figures in the history of Christianity.

The Story of Paul

Saint Paul wrote many letters which are now part of the New Testament. Thanks to these letters, we know more about him than we do about many other saints of the early Church. His story is written here in three chapters, so it can be read by different readers or at different times.

CHAPTER ONE

My name is Saul. I was born in Tarsus, a busy place not far from the blue Mediterranean Sea. Here, rugged mountain people came to sell goatskins; Persian traders led in camels carrying spices and perfumes for trading; and Roman soldiers, with their plumed helmets and sharp swords, guarded the roads. There I lived with my Jewish parents, who were descendants of the tribe of Benjamin. I spoke Greek, the language of Tarsus. I studied Hebrew as a very young child, so I could learn the sacred Scriptures and laws of my Jewish people.

I studied hard even then, because as my mother said, I never did things half-way. I decided I wanted to be a rabbi. "This is good," my father said. "You care deeply about people, and will dedicate yourself to Scripture and the law. I will send you to a fine instructor. But first, you must learn a trade to support your-self." So, from my father I learned tentmaking. He chuckled at my enthusiasm, but what was funny? If you are going to do something, do it well!

After that, I traveled all the way to the holy city of Jerusalem, to study under the great teacher Gamaliel. I plunged into this with all my heart. What a privilege it was to study Scripture with him! I vowed I would pass my learning on to everyone I could! I returned to Tarsus to teach. Then when I was a man of about thirty, I traveled back to Jerusalem once again. What I found disturbed me greatly.

There was a small group of Jews, Jews who observed the laws as I did, but who kept talking about a Jewish man named Jesus who had died a few years earlier. He had been crucified by the authorities. These Jews claimed he had risen from the dead. Imagine! They declared he was the Messiah, the one we had been longing for. This is outrageous, I thought. It must be stopped. One of these people, a man named Stephen, was blaspheming this way. Some Jewish leaders became so enraged that they threw stones at him, killing him. I watched it all. He had to die, I felt, for he was spreading untruths. That day, a persecution broke out against these followers of Jesus. Many hid, many scattered to other places. I vowed that I would seek them out and put an end to this thing. I began making plans.

CHAPTER TWO

Everything in my life changed quite suddenly. Here is how it happened. As you know, I never do things halfway. When I vowed to stop this movement—the Way, as it was called—I began going into houses where I thought these followers were hiding, and dragged them out. Men or women…I did not care who they were if they were spreading these untruths. Those I found I had imprisoned. Oh, the screaming and crying I heard, but I kept on, for the law must be upheld!

Now, I knew that many people of the Way were in the city of Damascus. I went straight to the high priest, asking him for letters that would give me the right to capture people of the Way in Damascus and bring them to Jerusalem in chains. I began traveling with some companions. It was on the road to Damascus that my life changed.

It was a normal day until suddenly, a flash of light surrounded me! It was so bright, I fell to the ground, my eyes shut against it. A voice called out to me, "Saul, Saul, why do you persecute me?"

I began shaking, but I asked this voice, "Who are you, sir?"

"I am Jesus, the one you are persecuting," the voice said.

Jesus! I was trembling violently now. Here was the voice of the one who had died, the one others claimed had risen again! And, he was speaking to me! I found my voice once more. "What do you want me to do?"

"Go into the city. There you will be told what to do."

Then there was silence. My companions began whispering nervously, for they had heard Jesus' voice but had seen nothing. And now, opening my eyes, I could see nothing. I was completely blind! We traveled into Damascus, no longer the confident group intent on capture. I had to be led by the hand. For three days, I lived in the darkness of my soul. I took neither food nor drink. As I prayed, I came to understand that a man would come to help me. His name would be Ananias.

And Ananias arrived. What courage it must have taken for him to come to me! My reputation for hunting down followers of the Way was well known. "Brother Saul, Jesus, who appeared to you on your journey, has told me to restore your sight," he said, and he laid his hands upon me. Immediately, I could see! Ananias then baptized me; I was now one of the followers of the Way.

CHAPTER THREE

When I first heard about the Way, I felt that if it was wrong, I should do all in my power to stamp it out. After Jesus came to me, I knew I must do all in my power to spread the news of Jesus. My love for him burned like a fire in my heart.

At first, Peter and some other disciples distrusted me, of course, but then they saw that my change was sincere. I went straightaway to the synagogues, preaching that Jesus was the Son of God. The other Jews were confused by the change in me. Soon there was a plot against me. But good friends took me by night, put me in a basket, and lowered me over the walls of the city. I escaped, returning to Jerusalem. But I did not stay there.

For thirty years I have traveled about, bringing the news of Jesus' love to others. I acquired a new name—Paul. I crossed much of the Roman Empire during four journeys, traveling thousands of miles, often on foot. (You can read about my travels in the Acts of the Apostles, chapters 13–28.) Everywhere I met people and told them of Jesus. Then I would move on, leaving behind communities of believers. I worried about them, so I wrote them letters to encourage them.

It has been a good life, but it has been very hard, too. With Jesus' help, I have survived three shipwrecks, imprisonment, beatings, and robbers, as well as threats in cities, in deserts, and on the sea. I have been hungry, thirsty, and lonely. In my teaching, I have never abandoned my fellow Jews. I love them, but I have argued with them over the laws of the Jews, the laws I had upheld before. I tell them that it is Jesus' love that we must cling to, not the rules.

And I know that they are not the only ones Jesus loves and wants to join him in the Way. So I began baptizing Gentiles, non-Jews, who wanted to follow Jesus, too. I do not know where all this will lead, but I believe I have done what is right.

I am old now. I know my end is near, for a great fire rages in the city of Rome and vicious rumors claim it is Jesus' followers who set it. Some are looking for an excuse to persecute us, and I know I may not escape this time. However, I am certain that neither death nor life will be able to separate us from the love of God, which is in Jesus.

I know that I have fought the good fight. I have finished the race, and I have kept the faith. Now I look forward to receiving the crown of righteousness, which the Lord will give to me and to all who long for his coming.

Activities

Saint Paul is a pivotal figure in early Christianity. Introduce him to children in these ways.

1. Paul's extensive travel for his missionary work had a profound effect on the growth of Christianity. Help children begin to understand what an accomplishment this was by explaining the difficulties of travel in that time. Read an account of a shipwreck Paul survived in Acts 27:14–44. Then list places that Paul traveled to, such as Jerusalem, Rome, Cyprus, Damascus, and Crete. Challenge children to find these places on a map.

2. Paul's contribution to the New Testament is vast, and he is often quoted, especially 1 Corinthians 13:4–7. Find a few key passages from Paul's letters, and read them aloud. Discuss how these words from long ago still apply today. Explain that these passages are from the letters Paul refers to in the preceding story.

3. Saint Paul is so important a figure in the Catholic Church that he is recognized each year with two feast days: January 25 (the conversion of Paul) and June 29 (the feast of Saints Peter and Paul). Provide children with a book of feast days and find information about each day.

Timeline

Using the example of the timeline on page 3 or 4 as a guide, create the first-century segment of your timeline. Discuss aspects of Paul's story that would make good symbols for the timeline. Encourage children to research more about this century, or about other saints of this time, to add to your timeline.

You might want to incorporate these dates into your timeline: the gospel of Mark was written around the year 65 AD, Matthew's around 70, Luke, 75, and John, 95.

More saints of this century

Stephen (d.c. 36), Peter (d. 67), Mary Magdalene, Thomas, Martha, Andrew, Philip, James, Luke, Mark, Matthew, John, Titus (d.c. 94), Timothy (d.c. 97).

Perpetua & Felicity

Died c. 203

In the years between 100 and 200, Arabian ships sailed over the Indian Ocean. They carried silk, spices, and precious stones to be traded for glass and metal, pottery and cloth. Caravans traveled slowly across central Asia for trading, too, linking the vast empires of China and Rome. In the year 166, Emperor Huang-Ti received gifts from Emperor Marcus Aurelius.

This span of time would encompass the Roman Empire at its greatest extent, but as the century ebbed, the beginnings of a decline could be seen. The empire's road network stretched from northern Britannia to the edge of the Sahara, from the Straits of Gibraltar to the Persian Gulf, and gave passage over the Alps. These impressive roads were paved in three layers. Europe would not again see roads of this quality for another thousand years.

In the northern part of the empire, now known as Britain, frontier towns were forts, with inns for travelers, a bathhouse for relaxation, and houses for the families of the soldiers. The harsh climate made life hard, but supplies such as spices, salt, barley, ham, and venison were available. Life for those in the warmer areas of the empire was easier, particularly for the wealthy and the large middle class. Men and women dined together while reclining on couches, public baths were important meeting places, and theaters and circuses entertained free citizens. Elaborate buildings with balconies graced streets, though crowded apartments of the poor existed amid the beauty.

As always, religion was diverse throughout the world. Buddhism was weakening in India, as Hinduism became stronger. The Romans worshiped a variety of gods, though citizens in the northern parts kept to Celtic practices. The Jewish people lived in scattered communities. Some revolted against Roman rule in 132, wanting to establish an independent state. They captured Jerusalem, but three years later this effort was crushed and many of its leaders killed.

The group calling themselves Christians

had increased greatly since the previous century. Small communities were scattered in Syria, Asia Minor, Greece, Italy, Spain, Gaul, and northern Africa. They made the Roman officials very nervous. Would the Christians incite a rebellion? They did refuse to act as soldiers, saying they were pacifists. These Christians rejected all worship of Roman gods—what were they, atheists? They would not even put a few grains of incense into the flame burning for the emperor! They were disloyal and a threat. The Roman gods might not take kindly to any tolerance of this behavior, and then everyone would suffer.

These fears led to two hundred years of persecution in which thousands of Christians died for their faith. The persecution was not continuous, and in times of tolerance the Church grew rapidly. In the worst of times, the tremendous courage of the martyrs only seemed to encourage others to be baptized.

Despite the fears and chaos this must have caused early Christians, the Church was slowly organizing itself. By the beginning of the second century, all the Christian Scriptures were intact. By the end, two major annual festivals were celebrated: Pascha, which was like our observance of Holy Week, and Pentecost. In the years between, large numbers of small communities sprang up and grew in love and support for one another through joy, sorrow, and constant fear.

It was into one of these communities in northern Africa that two young women, Perpetua and Felicity, chose to be baptized, placing themselves in a dangerous position. The story of their faith and martyrdom is known to us because Perpetua kept a diary during the days of her imprisonment, right up to her death. This account of life in early Christian times has been treasured among Christians for centuries.

We celebrate the feast day of Perpetua and Felicity on March 7.

The Story of Perpetua & Felicity

While the topic of martyrdom is a painful one, the early martyrs' role is significant to the history of our church. It is important that today's young Christians understand the courage and faith shown by the martyrs. Here the story is told through Perpetua's father, a non-Christian mentioned in Perpetua's diary, as he explains to his grandson the circumstances of Perpetua's death. It could be read by one person, or an additional person could read the child's lines.

The man called his grandson to him. "Come, sit down here by me. You are old enough now to understand why your mother died when you were a baby," he said softly. When the child was sitting close to him, the man asked, "Do you know what it means to be a Christian?"

The boy nodded. "Grandmother has told me. And I know many Christians."

The grandfather went on, "Then you may know that people can be arrested just because they are suspected of being Christian. Here, in Carthage, it is only once in a while that someone is imprisoned. The soldiers do this so others will be too frightened to become Christian. It was one of those times that the soldiers came here. They took with them your mother—she was only twenty-two then—leaving your grandmother and uncle who were also Christians. They also took one of our slave women, Felicity, who, like your mother, was studying to become Christian. Their teacher, Saturus, volunteered to go with them."

"He was very brave," the child said.

"Your mother was very brave, too. I want you to know that of all the hard things that happened to her, the hardest was leaving you behind. And Felicity was about to give birth. They waited until her child was born, then imprisoned her, too."

"Her daughter lives here," the boy said quietly.

"Yes, of course, we care for her, too, for she is motherless, like you. When they were in prison, I visited. As I am not a Christian, I could visit safely. How my heart ached to see my daughter in a cruel prison. How frightened I was to know she faced certain death! I pleaded with her. I begged her to say she was not a Christian. It seemed a small price to pay in order to live!"

"What did she say, Grandfather?"

"I remember she answered me so calmly. 'Father,' she said. 'Do you see this water jug standing here? Could one call it by another name than what it is? Well, in the same way, I cannot be called by any other name than what I am—a Christian.'"

The boy shifted slightly as his grandfather wiped his eyes.

Then the man went on, "I still begged her, but she said, 'It shall happen as God shall choose, for assuredly we depend not on our own power but on the power of God.' I knew then that I would never change her mind. Her faith in this Jesus was stronger than her fear. I did not see her again. She, Felicity, Saturus, and three others died soon after that day."

"I wish she was here," the little boy said. "But I am proud of her. Grandfather, what is so good about being Christian?"

The grandfather smiled a little, and took the child's hand in his. "I wondered about that many times after my Perpetua's death. From what your grandmother tells me, Christians love each other as no other group does. They take care of one another. Orphans and widows, the sick, the dying, the frightened, the imprisoned—no one is forgotten. Everyone is loved, everyone is important. And then there is Jesus. That man, they call him God. Even though he died many years ago, people seem to think of him as if he were here now."

"Grandfather, do you think I should become a Christian?"

The man gently squeezed his grandson's hand. "That is for you to decide when you are older. It is a question I ask myself all the time. But I know what your mother would say to both of us."

Activities

1. Saint Perpetua has been compared to Anne Frank. Both were young, were imprisoned, and died for their religious beliefs and lifestyles. Both wrote of their experiences while in captivity, and their writings had a tremendous effect on the world after their deaths.

   Anne's actual diary is best suited for ages thirteen and older, but there are several excellent books for younger children that tell Anne's story. Share one of these and lead a discussion about Perpetua's and Anne's lives and deaths. Compare the persecution of the early Christians and the persecution of the Jews in the mid 1900s.

2. Consider reading the book *Twenty and Ten,* by Claire Huchet Bishop, to your class. It is a very short chapter book, based on the true story of Christian children in France who sheltered Jewish children during World War II.

3. In meeting each other in public, early Christians would quickly draw a simple outline of a fish in dirt or sand, then cover it up, to communicate that they were indeed Christian. This symbol remained secret while it was necessary, but is now a common sign of Christianity. Encourage children to draw and decorate such a symbol to be put on their own door, desk, or bulletin board.

Timeline

Using the information at the beginning of this chapter and in the story, add the second-century segment to your timeline.

More Saints of This Century

Ignatius of Antioch (d.c. 107); Justin (d. 165); Irenaeus (c. 130-220).

Anthony of Egypt

251-356

In the year 211, the Roman Emperor Septimius Severus died. It was a Roman custom to give divine status to their emperors who died with heirs to succeed them. This called for a public ceremony of religious ritual and festivity, called "deification." Though the actual body was buried, a wax replica was made, and displayed on an ivory bed in the palace entrance. Songs of thanksgiving were sung, and wealthy citizens dressed in mourning clothes assembled. An eagle was released, which was to carry the emperor's soul to heaven. After the ceremony concluded, the emperor was worshiped with the rest of the gods.

Christianity was still a very young religion, growing within the confines of Roman rule and religious beliefs. In the year 200, the bishop of Rome, the Pope, was recognized as the head of western Christendom. Nevertheless, fifty years later, emperor worship was made compulsory in the Roman empire. Persecution of Christians was carried out in mid-century, when such well-known martyrs as Saints Agnes and Agatha died.

Christians lived among the many levels of social classes. Most citizens of the vast empire, of course, did enjoy amenities quite astounding for that time in history. A wide variety of occupations, such as wine merchants, greengrocers, bakers, millers, butchers, and blacksmiths were needed.

Among the workers were scribes, since many people could not read or write. A scribe living in what is today known as Germany used a bronze pen and ink to write on vellum, parchment made of calf or lamb skin. His son practiced his writing on a wooden tablet covered with wax. With an ivory stylus, he would write his letters, then heat the tablet to smooth the wax again. Later, he could play with glass marbles, or pretend to be a Roman soldier. At home, they would dine on meatballs made of sheep brains, eggs, and herbs.

Children in Roman Britain played many games that are still played today, such as hide-and-seek, leap frog, and hopscotch. A long length of wool wound tightly around a smooth stone created a ball that bounced. Small boys had kites, tops, and play chariots, while little girls had dolls with jointed arms. Both boys and girls played on swings and see-saws.

At age fourteen, a wealthy boy would perform a religious ritual, a rite of passage, by placing his toys and childhood treasures on the altar of his household god, adding the good luck charm he had worn since birth. Girls had a similar ritual, also about age fourteen, on the night before their wedding.

Of course, thousands of men were soldiers, and a huge number of people were in agriculture, many of whom were slaves. The slave class was made up of poor people and those captured when other states were conquered.

For most of this century after Severus' death, the people of the Roman empire lived under the rule of a series of weaker emperors. The empire's immense size made ruling it increasingly difficult, and groups of great warriors, called Barbarians by the Romans, were pressing in from the north.

Other unrest prevailed: Athens, Corinth, and Sparta were sacked by Goths, and Barbarians took over southwest Korea, pushing out Chinese colonies there. Toward the end of the third century, a Roman emperor named Diocletian emerged, who was a brilliant administrator. He divided the empire into two parts, ruling the eastern part himself.

Halfway through this century, a child named Anthony was born in Egypt. His parents were wealthy and Christian. He would, as a young man, embrace Christianity wholeheartedly and turn his back on his wealth. He lived one hundred and five years (forty-nine years in the third century, fifty-six in the fourth century), the majority of them spent in solitude and prayer. Anthony of Egypt is remembered today as the Father of Monks, a pioneer in Christian monasticism. His feast day is January 17.

The Story of Anthony of Egypt

Choose five readers to tell Saint Anthony's story. Each will read twice.

First Reader   Saint Anthony was born a wealthy child in Egypt, less than three hundred years after Jesus lived. Anthony's parents died when he was about eighteen, leaving him to care for his sister and their riches.

Second Reader   One day, Anthony was in church. He heard a gospel reading from Matthew in which Jesus said to a rich young man, "Go, sell what you own, and give the money to the poor." All the way home, Anthony thought about this. It seemed as if Jesus were saying those words just for him. Then he made a decision: he would give away everything except just what he and his sister needed.

Third Reader   Soon after this, Anthony heard another Scripture passage from Matthew: "Do not worry about tomorrow." Again, Anthony made a decision. He found a group of holy women to care for his sister, left what money she would need, and said good-bye to her. He gave away the rest of his money and walked out into the desert.

Fourth Reader   Anthony longed to know God deeply. He felt he needed to be all alone in a quiet place. Sometimes he lived in small huts, sometimes in caves, and sometimes he even slept in cemeteries. Each day he prayed, studied, and worked in his small garden. Anthony had become a monk. That word comes from a Greek word meaning "alone."

Fifth Reader   Wanting to live as simply as possible, he chose to eat only small amounts of food. He did not sleep long hours, either. Anthony was tired, hungry, and thirsty often. Then there were dangers from animals: lions, crocodiles, snakes, and scorpions!

First Reader   For years, Anthony lived by himself. Sometimes, however, it did not seem to Anthony that he was alone. He had dreams and visions of frightening things. Still, Anthony went on with his prayer, believing he was doing just what God asked of him. He remained healthy and happy.

Second Reader   Now he felt ready to be with a few people again. Some men came to him, hearing of his holiness. They asked him to lead them in a new life, one like his. Anthony agreed. Since he did not like stately buildings, the new monks lived in small, separate huts. They came together to pray each day. This was the first Christian monastery, and it was called the Fayum.

Third Reader   The monks found that Anthony was filled with stories and wisdom. Someone wrote down the teachings of Anthony. Soon others arrived to stay for a short time and learn from Anthony. They all could see the happiness he felt, for his face almost seemed to shine. They knew, too, that this was because Anthony so loved God and knew that God loved him.

Fourth Reader   Back in the crowded world, far from Anthony's monastery, Christians were being imprisoned and killed because they loved Jesus. Anthony felt he should go back to town, to die for Jesus. How hard it must have been for Anthony to leave his peaceful life! Still, Anthony boldly went to Alexandria. He was never arrested. Anthony realized God wanted him to live out a long life as a monk. He went back to the Fayum.

Fifth Reader   When Anthony was eighty-four years old, he once again traveled to Alexandria to teach about Jesus. He worked miracles there. Then, he settled near the Red Sea, again by himself. He took care of his pets and worked in his garden. He died peacefully when he was one hundred and five years old.

Activities

For all of us living in today's busy, noisy world, Anthony's life shows us that Christians need to cultivate some form of simplicity and solitude in our lives so we can be open to prayer and God's call.

1. Encourage children to have some "Anthony time," that is, quiet time for prayer. Provide a prayer space in your classroom or home. Can your space allow for a light cloth to be hung temporarily around it? Perhaps a corner with a rug can serve. Can an area where supplies are kept be covered by sheets? Once you have a space, place a small table there, and set this with a tablecloth, candle, a cross or image of Jesus, and a children's Bible. A small notebook for written prayer petitions could also be there.

   Tell the children about the prayer space. Speak of the importance of silence and prayer, of listening for the quiet voice of God within each person. Tell them that this prayer space is for quiet only, like the places where Anthony lived. While they are there, they may read the Bible, pray, or write in a journal, or add their prayer petitions to the notebook. Provide a time when children may enter the space in small numbers or individually.

2. Suggestions can be given to children for creating such a space in their own bedrooms. Speak from time to time during regular group prayer of the importance of nurturing the quiet center each of us has within us.

Timeline

Using the information at the beginning of this chapter and in the story, add the third-century segment to your timeline.

More Saints of This Century

Callistus I (d.c. 223); Pontian and Hippolytus (d. 235); Agatha (d.c. 251); Sebastian (c. 257-288); Cornelius (d. 253); Cyprian (d. 258); Agnes (d.c. 258); Sixtus (d. 258); Cosmas and Damien (d. 303).

Lucy   d. 304
Nicholas   280-343
Martin of Tours   316-397
Augustine   354-430
Melania   382-439

The fourth century brought momentous change for Christianity. In the beginning of the century, Christians were a persecuted group, imprisoned and killed. By the time the fifth century was dawning, Christianity had become the official religion of the Roman Empire. This would have reverberations for centuries to come. How did this all come about? Much is due to a man named Constantine.

Years of incompetent emperors in the vast Roman Empire had left it crumbling. Then Diocletian came into power. Though an excellent administrator, he was anti-Christian, and in 303, he ordered a general persecution of Christians. Once again, the young Church was tormented by violence and repression.

When Diocletian abdicated two years later,

Constantine emerged as a leader. He was a man who was willing to worship any god who would grant him victory. Before a particularly difficult battle, Constantine had a dream or vision that he would conquer through a sign of Christ. He had his soldiers put the first two Greek letters of Christ's name on their banners and shields. When they won, Constantine was convinced. He honored the Son of God in thanksgiving, much to the amazement of the Roman senate.

Constantine shared imperial power with a general named Licinius. In June of 313, they issued the Edict of Toleration, granting freedom to Christians in the Roman Empire. No longer could Christians be punished legally for practicing their religion.

But it also meant the emperor could be involved with Church matters. In 325, he called the first ecumenical council of the Church, the Council of Nicaea. This meeting dealt with significant issues, such as the Arian heresy which would haunt the Church for years to come. The Nicaean creed was formulated there, too. By 330, the Church of Saint Peter was erected in Rome. But Rome itself was in decay, and Constantine moved the capital to Byzantium, near Asia Minor. In 337, the great Christian emperor lay on his deathbed, and requested baptism. Like others of the fourth through sixth centuries, he believed that forgiveness was given only once, so he waited until the end for that forgiveness.

There were still short periods of persecution in this century, but for the most part, the Church had status: it was given lands, clergy were not taxed, and some bishops ranked high in public life. By the end of the century, the Roman empire was in definite decline. The emperors then spent most of their time trying to defend the frontiers from the invading Franks, Goths, Vandals, Huns, and Visigoths. But Christianity was on the rise, for in 395, it was declared the official religion of the empire. Yet it was a far different Church than the one the wandering band of apostles had begun.

Many saints lived in this extraordinary time. Lucy (feast day December 13) died for her faith; Bishop Nicholas (December 6) was imprisoned for his; Martin (November 11) forsook a military career to spread Christianity; Augustine (August 28) resisted becoming a Christian before turning into one of the Church's greatest spokesmen; and Melania (December 31) cast off tremendous Roman wealth for simplicity.

They shared the same century, but lived in different decades, places, and circumstances. It is to them that we turn to learn of this time.

Five Voices of the Fourth Century

Choose six readers to represent the narrator, Lucy, Nicholas, Martin, Augustine, and Melania.

Narrator   Imagine with me the year 304. Christians were being imprisoned and often killed for their faith, for Emperor Diocletian had ordered a persecution of Christians. Despite fear, many held firmly to their faith. Now we will meet a very young woman who faced this hostile time.

Lucy   My name is Lucy. I am a young Christian, about to step into adult life. However, I think that I will be asked to give up this life for Jesus. I am from the island of Sicily, where it is against Roman law to be Christian. But I love Jesus and believe in his love. One reason I believe is that when my mother was ill, I prayed, and she became well again.

Even though we Christians need to be quiet about who we are, we have learned many ways to live as Jesus asks. I vowed I would never marry, as I wanted to work only for Christianity. My family, however, had already betrothed me to a young man. When I refused to marry, he was greatly angered. Just yesterday, he accused me of being a Christian, and I was dragged before the governor. Now, imprisoned, I await my fate. I am frightened. I have known others who came here, only to die. But I am comforted knowing Jesus will be with me, no matter what happens. I pray I can die as bravely as those who have gone before me.

Narrator   Saint Lucy did die bravely, and has become a greatly loved saint. Because her name means "light" and her feast day falls in December, the darkest time of the year, there are many customs which feature Lucy as a bringer of light. She is often pictured as a young woman in a white dress with a red sash, a crown of evergreens and lit candles on her head. Her Advent feast day reminds us that Christ, the Light of the World, is coming.

Now imagine a tall bishop standing before you, in the year 325.

Nicholas   My name is Nicholas of Asia Minor. My wealthy parents taught me to be generous, so when they died, I gave away my inheritance. I don't speak much about this, but others seem very interested in it. I entered the priesthood while in my teens and became a bishop before I was thirty—thus the nickname "boy bishop." I endured prison under Emperor Diocletian. Apparently, God did not have martyrdom in his plans for me, for though I worked in prison to keep up the spirits of others there with me, I lived to tell the tale.

All of that has changed now. To our amazement and relief, the present emperor, Constantine, has embraced Christ! We are free now, and the Church is growing rapidly. If that is not amazing enough, the emperor has built churches, and has even called an important meeting in the city of Nicaea. I am attending now, along with bishops from Egypt, Palestine, Syria, Greece, and of course, Asia Minor. There are over two hundred of us, and the emperor attends our meetings. We have long discussions, particularly about the teachings of a priest named Arius who claims that Jesus is not God. We call this the Arian heresy. Oh, the long, heated debates, the frustration! But this is most important work, and I am honored to be part of it.

Narrator   Saint Nicholas lived a long life, working for his people as bishop. Some say he was a calm man unless there was an injustice; then he could spring like a lion. After he died, miracles were done in his name, many involving children. These, and his habit of quietly giving gifts have led to his famous reputation. You know him, perhaps, by the name of Santa Claus.

About ten years after this council, an eighteen-year-old Roman soldier was transferred to a camp in what you call France.

Martin   Hello! My name is Martin, and I am in the Roman army. I am deeply troubled these days. My father is a soldier, and even when I was little, I knew sons of soldiers must become soldiers. Still, when I was ten, I studied to become a Christian. My parents were upset and did not allow me to be baptized, but I did not forget what I learned.

The other day, something happened that I must tell you about. It is a particularly cold winter this year and I was wearing my woolen uniform cloak. I was on horseback, and when I reached the gates of the city, I saw a poor man standing there, dressed in rags. He was begging for food or money, and as I had neither at the time, I took off my cloak and my sword. I cut the cloak in two, and put one piece around the shoulders of the poor man. That night, I had a dream in which the beggar came to me, still clad in my cloak. When he turned around, he had the face of Christ! I awoke troubled but excited. I want to be baptized! But then what? Followers of Christ do not hurt others, yet I am a soldier! How can I lead others into battle? I have some big decisions to make.

Narrator Martin of Tours followed his heart. He was baptized soon after his dream, then worked for several years to be released from the army. He became a hermit for a time, as he wished to avoid hearing of the Arian heresy, but Martin was destined to be a leader. Soon he was the head of a large monastery. He also taught people in nearby towns, who then wanted him as their bishop. Martin agreed very reluctantly, but did these duties well. By this time, the government was giving bishops land and wealth, but Martin lived simply, founding more monasteries and reaching out to hundreds of people. His reputation was great, and when he died, he became the first person to be honored as a saint who had not died as a martyr.

While Martin was busy teaching others about Jesus, a child was born who would resist his own Christianity, and still become one of the greatest Christian writers of all time. The year was 389.

Augustine My name is Augustine. These are corrupt times. All around me there is tremendous wealth, yet our great empire is falling apart. Many people look for empty pleasure in this false wealth.

I was a fortunate child. My mother, Monica, a Christian, did everything a mother could do to provide me with a Christian education. But though I was quick to learn, I found the study of Christianity boring. Now I knew that not long ago, people actually died for this religion, but it did not seem to hold anything for me. Instead, I lived wildly, like others of this time, seeking pleasure that left me nothing. Then I met Bishop Ambrose. I kept going back to hear him preach. I began having nagging doubts about my life, but would not give up my wild ways. The feelings grew stronger, and one day, I was in great anguish when I heard a voice—I do not know whose—say, "take up and read." I began to read Scripture once again. All at once, I knew I would follow Jesus, and I was at peace. I have been baptized, and now I study Scripture and pray. And I write. There are many things to consider: why is there so much sin, and yet so much grace, God's love, to help us resist the sin? Also, Christians have always avoided war, they are pacifists. Is this right, I wonder? Oh, I must think about and write of all of this!

Narrator   Saint Augustine became a priest, then bishop of Hippo, in North Africa. He was a remarkable teacher, and he did write and write! Augustine was named a Doctor of the Church, that is, a person who is especially wise and a great teacher of our faith. Augustine was a very complicated man, who lived and wrote with intensity. Centuries after his death people still read his books, so he is still teaching and raising questions in people.

As Augustine was writing and the century drawing to a close, a young woman chose Christian simplicity over Roman wealth.

Melania   Greetings! My name is Melania, and I am from Rome. I think I will not stay here long, however, for we fear invaders. My husband, Pinian, and my mother speak of fleeing, perhaps to North Africa. My life has had so many changes; however, I do not fear more. I was born into a wealthy Christian family. I wanted to remain single and spend my life in prayer and good works. But my family insisted I marry when I was fourteen. Pinian and I had two children, but sadly, both died as babies. It was then that Pinian agreed that my first choice of life might be the right one. We needed to be rid of our great wealth. We freed our eight thousand slaves, sold our many large houses and lands, and gave away the money. We could then begin to live simply as Jesus did, and reach out to others. I can use my skills in Latin and Greek when we need money. There is much to do in Jesus' name.

Narrator   Saint Melania the Younger (her grandmother was Saint Melania the Elder) and family did flee Rome a few years later. They went first to North Africa, where they were greatly involved with the Church, and befriended Augustine. As part of her work, Melania started monasteries there and near Jerusalem. These saints and many others helped create a better world in the fourth century.

Activities

1. Help children research the types of clothing worn by people of various classes of the Roman Empire in the fourth century.

2. Have them create symbols for each saint in this story.

3. Make posters with the names and dates of these saints, and have children draw pictures of them, based on their research of the clothing, or draw the symbols, on the posters. When reading the parts of the story, have one child hold up the poster for the "saint" that is speaking.

Timeline

Using the information at the beginning of this chapter and in the story, add the fourth-century segment to your timeline.

More Saints of This Century

Hilary (c.315-368), Monica (c.322-387), Basil the Great (329-379), Gregory Nazianzen (329-390), Ambrose (340-397), Jerome (345-420).

Brigid of Ireland
430-525

If there had been television newscasts in the fifth century, no doubt the ongoing story would have been the migration of people all over the world. The Incas had established themselves on the Pacific coast of South America. Pacific Islanders had reached Easter Island and Hawaii by the year 400; different islands in that part of the world developed different cultures over the next centuries.

In Asia, the Mongol Huns were on the march westward, in search of new lands to settle, and the Japanese conquered parts of Korea. All over Europe and into Africa, various migrating groups, called "the Barbarians" by the Romans, were invading lands new to them in an effort to find food, land, and markets. Though they had been a threat to Romans already, the momentum of the invasion grew as the empire collapsed.

In 410, Rome was invaded by the Visigoths. By 476, the last emperor of the Roman Empire in the west stepped down, and that date is considered the official end of that great empire.

As the empire declined, the numbers of Roman soldiers in far-flung places also declined. Struggles for power and land sprang up in many places. The Classical Age was over, and the so-called Dark Ages had begun.

The Christian Church, while still relatively small from a human standpoint, was the one point of stability for those whose lives it touched. It emerged into leadership by default: many Christian leaders were well-educated in a time when education was not common. Some were capable organizers. They were able to implement the well-developed system of Roman law. Barbarians invading Christian lands were looking for a place to settle and farm. A system of laws would be needed eventually, and Church officials became the logical leaders in this.

Into this picture came Saint Leo. Around 440, Leo was elected pope. For twenty-one years, Leo led the church in a gentle and scholarly way, in an age that was neither. He dealt with the Arian heresy as well as other heresies. His papacy helped shape the role which the pope plays to this day, incorporating statesman, spiritual leader, and administrator. A profound prayer life sustained him through these challenges. It enabled him to meet yet another challenge: Attila the Hun.

In 451, Italy was invaded by the Huns, who burned cities and killed entire populations. When the Huns headed for Rome, the emperor ordered Leo to meet Attila and his troops. He went, dressed not in protective armor but in priestly garb. Attila agreed not to enter Rome, in exchange for an annual tribute.

Far to the north of all this activity lived the Celts, skilled ironworkers who made intricate jewelry, bronze mirrors, and decorated shields. They mostly worshiped their gods of the sea and forest, but Christianity had begun to seep in. Into this scenario came Patrick, a teen from Britain who was captured and enslaved by the Irish for six years. After his escape, he became a priest and then a bishop, returning to Ireland, where he converted tens of thousands of people and ordained hundreds of priests.

In this time of folk religion mixed with Christianity, a time when legend and fact intertwined, a girl-child was born to a slave mother and her chieftain master. She was called Brigid, and she was destined to capture the hearts of the Irish people, as well as many others, with her indomitable spirit and profound holiness. Her feast day is February 1.

The Story of Brigid of Ireland

Following is Brigid's story. You may read it, or choose several children to read it. Everyone else can be the chorus.

Reader 1   My name is Brigid, and I lived in Ireland a long time ago, when Saint Patrick was preaching and teaching the message of Christ. I took that message very seriously, especially about giving to those who were needy and hungry. My mother, Brocca, and I were slaves. I worked in the dairy, milking cows, skimming cream, making butter. If I saw people who were hungry, I gave them milk or butter. Oh, the fuss that was made then! How did I dare give away the master's food? Well, I did dare, for he had enough, and these others did not. I didn't care if those in charge fussed. I gave milk away time and again. Hungry people began coming to me, and I always found something to give to them. Finally I was dismissed, for those in charge had had it with me.

Chorus   God will provide for us; yes, God will provide.

Reader 2   I was free! Free to serve God as I wished. I took vows and became a nun. With seven other women, I started a convent. We baked bread, grew fruits, milked cows, and cooked to feed the hungry who came to our door. But sometimes, it was not just the hungry who came.

One day, after we had sliced the last loaf of bread, picked the last pear, scrambled the last egg, and poured the last drop of milk, word came that seven—seven!—bishops were on their way, to visit and to eat with us. The other sisters were aghast. "What can we do? We have nothing left, nothing at all!" they exclaimed.

Chorus   God will provide for us; yes, God will provide.

Reader 3   "God will provide," I said confidently. After all, I had once given water to an ill woman. Before our very eyes, it had turned to milk, and the sick woman recovered. Often I had filled the butter jar half full, asked God to help, and sure enough, it would soon be brimming with butter. "Go ask the hens kindly if we might have an egg or two," I said. "See if the cow might be persuaded to give a bit more milk, and ask the trees if they might have more fruit ripen tonight."

The sisters went off, and I went into the kitchen, stirred up the fire, and lo, what did I see! In the oven were loaves of hot, crusty bread, just waiting to be pulled out. The sisters returned with eggs, milk, apples, and pears. Yes, it was a miracle, and a tasty one at that! The bishops feasted, and life, all miraculous life, went on.

Chorus   God will provide for us; yes, God will provide.

Reader 4   But my duties expanded. I began a monastery under a large oak tree. We called it *Cil dara,* or "church of the oak." Men as well as women joined us, and it became an important center for learning. As part of it, I began an art school, where the skill of illuminating manuscripts was practiced—with beautiful results. We had no printing presses, no copy machines or computers. Books were made by hand. Books were still a rather new idea, for scrolls had been used until about one hundred years ago. The artists at Cil dara would write the story of Jesus in careful, fancy handwriting, and then decorate each page with symbols in breathtaking paintings in reds, blues, greens, and golds. Angels, eagles, lions, and peacocks danced across those pages! Oh, they were a magnificent sight to behold. We held the word of God very sacred and tried to make these books worthy of it. Some people, seeing the beauty of these pages, said they could not be the work of human hands alone.

"Brigid prays, and as she does, angels come and tell the artists what to do," some claimed. And I laugh and continue to pray.

Chorus   God will provide for us; yes, God will provide.

Reader 5   The monastery grew very large and there was always a great deal of work. Still, what was most important to me was to go out to others less fortunate than I, bringing food, clothing, and medicines. And to help me do that, I had a chariot to ride. All that was a long time ago, but I am still remembered and loved, especially by the Irish people, and I am delighted that you are hearing about me today!

Chorus   God will provide for us; yes, God will provide.

Activities

Brigid's monastery was known for its illuminated manuscripts. In honor of Saint Brigid, learn about these works of art and create some of your own. Find books showing examples of them, such as **The Book of Kells** *by Bernard Meehan, or* **The Books of Kells** *by Peter Brown. (The Book of Kells, an illuminated manuscript of the Gospels, produced during the seventh and ninth centuries, is thought to have been preceded by the Book of Kildare, most likely produced in Brigid's time.)*

1. On a sheet of white 8 1/2 inch by 11 inch paper, make a border by laying a ruler along each edge and tracing around it. Within the border, make a letter (such as your first or last name initial) so the edges touch the border. Color the letter with black crayon. Then divide the remaining space between the letter and border into smaller areas, filling these with other colors (traditional are red, blue, and green.) Decorate the border as you like. All coloring should be solid and heavy. Then using a cloth or paper towel, go over the drawing several times with a solvent such as nail polish remover, which will dissolve some of the wax and leave the color. Hang these in a window for a stained-glass effect.

2. Provide gold-colored pencils and regular colored pencils. Have children choose a favorite Scripture passage. On paper, using a thin black marker, make the first letter of the first word large and ornate, then print the rest of the verse as nicely as possible. Decorate around the big letter and in the borders with the gold pencil and other colors, particularly with religious symbols.

Timeline

Using the information at the beginning of this chapter and in the story, add the fifth-century segment to your timeline.

More Saints of This Century

Cyril of Alexandria (376-444); Patrick (389-461); Peter Chrysologus (406-450); Leo the Great (d.461); Genevieve (422-512).

Benedict

480-550

Scholastica

480-543

In the sixth century, the Anasazi people lived in homes partly underground and built dams to conserve the scarce water of Arizona, New Mexico, Utah, and Colorado. In the mud that formed in the dammed-up areas, they planted maize, beans, and squash, and supplemented these foods with wild game, nuts, seeds, and berries gathered from the wild. In the winter, they must have been a magnificent sight in their cloaks made of rabbit skins and feathers.

Far to their north, in the lands around the Great Lakes, lived villages of the Hopewell peoples. To the south, in what we call Mexico, a settlement called Teotihuacan had grown from its ancient beginnings in 150 BC to a city of 200,000 with streets and a marketplace, where craftspeople, farmers, traders, and their families lived in compounds around courtyards. Even further south, the Mayans were flourishing in Guatemala.

Across the sea, centuries of migration from western Africa brought about settlements in southern Africa. By the 500s, life for these people centered around small villages, where they cultivated cereal crops, kept sheep, cattle, and goats, smelted iron, and made pottery. The wealthy and powerful kingdom of Axum, now Ethiopia, had many Christian citizens by this time. Christianity would remain strong there for centuries.

Buddhism reached Japan by mid-century, and in 570, a child was born whose beliefs and leadership would later shake the Christian world. His name was Muhammad. But this Christian world had challenges enough during this time. In the eastern part, a great diplomat named Justinian was the emperor. One of the most influential men of the early Middle Ages (sometimes called the Dark Ages), his actions kept the eastern half of the Roman empire alive until the 1400s.

During Justinian's reign, from 527-565, the Church reached a high point in the East, especially in Syria, Greece, Iraq, Lebanon, Jordan,

Egypt, Albania, Turkey, and southern Russia. There were clashes, however, between Justinian and the West, where areas of the disintegrating empire were ruled by Arian kings. By this time, the term "catholic," meaning "universal," was being used to describe the church legally recognized by the Roman empire, which did not include the Arians. Other heresies challenged the Catholic Church, as well. Life in western Europe was still affected by the contrast between the vast wealth of some and the poverty of others, the overthrow of rulers, the lack of stability, the widespread fear, and the immoral lifestyles.

As the sixth century opened, a woman named Scholastica and her twin brother Benedict had just reached adulthood. Born into a distinguished family in central Italy, their lives would have offered them certain privileges, but they both chose more demanding paths.

Benedict's life had a profound effect on thousands of others in the years and even centuries following. When he was abbot of a monastery he founded in Monte Cassino, he wrote a Rule for his monks there. Now called the Rule of Saint Benedict, this Rule set a standard for western monastic tradition, being the guidelines used in nearly all the European monasteries founded between the sixth and eleventh centuries. So great was Benedict's impact that he was later given credit for saving European civilization during the Middle Ages, and was thus named patron of all of Europe.

Scholastica's life is less documented. The similarities of their choices, however, and the regular contact between them reveal a strong bond and a supportive relationship, which in turn benefitted the Christian world. Scholastica's feast day is February 10; Benedict's is July 11.

The Story of Benedict & Scholastica

This story is written in the form of letters from Benedict to Scholastica. You might have a girl/young woman read them as if she has just received them as letters, or have a boy/young man read them as if he were in the process of writing them. Or choose a boy and a girl, with the readers taking turns.

My dear twin sister Scholastica,

Greetings to you and to the rest of the family! I am settled now in Rome, receiving the education our father desires. While I am grateful to him for this opportunity, I find Rome, and even my school, a difficult place to be. All around me there is evil and selfishness. I find little concern for the poor people of Rome, yet fear is common among all the classes of people. The other students here live wild, undisciplined lives. I have found no one who tries to live as Christ teaches us in Scripture.

Scholastica, you and I are seventeen now, an age when we should be enthusiastic about what lies ahead of us. But I cannot be enthusiastic, for I see only unhappiness for myself unless I find another way of life. Perhaps I will give away my inheritance. I am also considering leaving all of this to live near Subiaco, about fifty miles south of Rome. I have been told by a holy man that there is a cave there, called Aniotal's cave, where I could live as a hermit. I would be removed from this world, free to work and pray in my own way. I wish I could talk with you to see what you think of this.

Pray for me, as I consider this great change.

Benedict

Dear Scholastica,

I am writing in case you have heard frightening things about me. I want to assure you that I am fine, and once again at Subiaco. My three years there as a hermit were good ones for me. I prayed and worked daily. Then, as you know from our last visit together, I was asked to become abbot of the monastery at Vicovaro. I tried hard, setting rules that I thought would benefit the monks that were there. But some of the monks thought my rules too strict. One in particular must have been very angry with me, for he tried to poison my wine! But God protected me, and all is well.

I have left Vicovaro, and now write to you from my old place. It is not the same, however, as other monks come seeking me in my solitude. They too have elected me abbot, and I pray things will go better. I have many thoughts about how best to lead these men. I pray over it constantly. I look forward to our next visit, for I want to speak with you about my plans, and hear your ideas.

Please let me know when we can next meet.

Benedict

Dear Sister,

How I look forward to our yearly meeting! I have much to tell you of my work, but as always when we see each other, I hope we will speak of our prayer lives, and of God's plans for each of us. I do not want to wait until I see you to tell you that I continue to set up new monasteries.

I am settled now in one on top of Monte Cassino, about halfway between Rome and Naples. The monks here are ordinary folk, some are Goths, some are Romans, all are Christians now. We rarely need to go into the outside world, as we can supply ourselves with clothing, food, and shelter. And in the quiet scriptorium we copy books, which are so precious and need our protection. Our work is quite amazing. God must be with us!

Until I see you, God's blessings to you!

Benedict

Dear Scholastica,

We must be in touch more frequently now with our big plans! A community for women, only five miles from Monte Cassino! I feel God's hand in this work! The details I needed to work out are finished, and I await your letter about what you have accomplished. It will be good to be working with you as you lead this community. I feel God is calling you to do this work. I look forward to your next letter.

Benedict

Dear twin sister,

Even though it has not been long since our last visit, I want to write to you of my work. As I told you then, I am working very hard on the rules, or the Rule, for the monasteries, as well as for your convent. I have more to tell you now. I am basing it on Scripture. The first duty of all monks is to pray. Our motto will be *Ora et labora*, pray and work. Our prayer lives will be balanced with work: work that keeps the monastery going; work that enables us to take care of travelers, the poor, and the sick who come to us; work that will educate ourselves and others.

Of course, I am building on the traditions of great monks of long ago, such as Anthony of Egypt. I am also taking ideas from some eastern monasteries and modifying them according to my experiences. I feel this Rule must be one that helps monks stay healthy—some monks believe the path to holiness lies in too little food, too little sleep. I feel we monks will find holiness in using our talents and energy for the good of each other and of others who need us, not in denying ourselves the basic needs. And the Rule must be able to work in many situations, as I now have twelve small monasteries. As I work on it, I think of the different monks, and what each one's gifts are, and how they can be guided to best give of those gifts.

Pray for me in this work, as I pray your work with your community goes well.

Benedict

Dear Scholastica,

Soon it will be time for our yearly visit! I look forward to meeting at our usual meeting place, the house between my monastery and your convent. Many, many years have passed now since our birth. How much more of God's work can be done through us? Let us meet soon to talk of God's great love!

Your twin brother,

Benedict

Activities

1. Little is known about Saint Scholastica, but there is a delightful story about the last meeting between the siblings which shows the depth of Scholastica's relationship with God, as well as her great love for her brother. Many books of saints contain this story under her name. Encourage children to find it, and have one child read it aloud.

2. Can Benedict's work speak to children of today? We live in a chaotic era, where extreme busyness and lack of community are common. Discuss with your students the idea of ordering their days in ways similar to Benedict's monks. Talk about how great things can come from quiet times, how balance in life keeps people healthy. Discuss the following basic concepts from the Rule of Saint Benedict: a) each day is divided into times of prayer, study, work, and rest; b) everyone works; c) no one keeps personal possessions, so there is little envy and pride; d) each person should be gentle and forgiving with others; be generous to all strangers or those in need; each visitor is to be treated like Christ. Then, suggest that students write their own rule to try for a week. At your next meeting, discuss what they have learned from this process.

3. Give children—or have them find—definitions of unfamiliar words they may encounter in learning of these two saints (e.g. monastery, abbess, abbot, and scriptorium).

Timeline

Using the information at the beginning of this chapter and in the story, add the sixth-century segment to your timeline.

More Saints of This Century

Boethius (c. 480-524); John I (d. 526); David of Wales (520-589); Gregory the Great (c. 540-604).

Cuthbert

634-687

The seventh century had just begun when a Mayan man traveled along a jungle road in the Yucatan Peninsula. He carried beads, pendants, and some small figures made of jade, which he hoped to trade in the next village. He might find there pots made of long coils of clay, or carvings from shells and stones.

While most Mayans lived in villages, growing maize, chili peppers, beans, squash, and root crops, there were cities he would travel to where fifty thousand people lived. Nobles, priests, rulers, officials, and servants made up the population in these political and religious centers. In one of these cities, he encountered a priest who helped develop a calendar that showed when eclipses of the sun and moon would occur, and he was challenged to use a math system based on the number twenty. Inside the large, pyramid-shaped temples were painted walls. Outside, a game similar to soccer was being played by other Mayan men, the solid ball bumping up against these walls.

As the Mayan man traveled for trade, a man in China labored to rebuild the very old Great Wall. His anger flared as he watched some of his coworkers die because of the harsh conditions created by the ruler Yang Di. Rebellion would ensue, and Yang Di would die as a result. But in this vast land, the many Buddhist temples, shrines, and monasteries spread a peaceful atmosphere. Buddhism was now the main religion in Burma. In Korea, where Buddhism was already established as the religion of the ruling class, the Shilla dynasty came into power, the first of three dynasties that would shape Korea for centuries to come.

Great change was brewing in Arabia. In 610, a man named Muhammad in the city of Mecca had a vision. The angel Gabriel appeared, telling him of Allah's (God) commands and teachings. Muhammad passed these on to his companions, collecting the beliefs in a book called the Koran. Written in Arabic, this would become the holy book of Muhammad's followers, called Muslims. Muhammad accepted the Old Testament, and so Muslims shared many beliefs with Jews and

Christians. He respected Jesus as a great prophet, but not as God. Islam, as this new religion was called, taught belief in one God, a wonderful life after death, a strict moral code, prayer five times a day, and times of fasting. It would become a great challenge to the Christian world.

In less than a hundred years, Islam spread out from Mecca to become an empire that stretched from Spain to India. Syria, Palestine, and Egypt, which had witnessed the events of early Christianity, were now under Muslin rule. This happened through military conquest, the most rapid in history, but it spread rapidly for other reasons, too. The Muslims borrowed and improved upon the best ideas of the people they conquered, improving some societies, and imposing an order that brought a sense of safety to many places. Islam also held great appeal through promises of a paradise after death.

Many Christians in the conquered areas became Muslim, and just how far this new religion would spread was a question asked by many in western Europe. Those in western Europe began to forget that some of the places now under Muslim control were areas where Christianity had started, where the blood of martyrs had been spilled. And from the seventh century on, the Muslims separated what had been the East and West of the Roman Empire, affecting communication between Church leaders.

Many aspects of Christianity in the seventh century would be recognizable by Catholics today. The practice of daily Mass had begun, there was a general acceptance of seven sacraments, and people went to Mass on Sundays and observed feast days of favorite saints.

There were differences between the celebration of the Mass in the East and in the West. In the West, Mass was celebrated in Latin. In the East, it was often said in Greek, and the eucharistic celebration was held behind panels, keeping laypeople from seeing the liturgical action and fostering a sense of great mystery.

Struggles between Christianity and the Germanic tribes overrunning western Europe continued. Life was hard and often short for many people. Still, signs of Christ's light shone in numerous places. In France, a monk named Fiacre was offering hospitality along with home-grown vegetables and herbs to all who needed it. The young slave-turned-queen named Bathildis was aiding the spread of Christianity through her position. Isidore of Seville was turning Spain into a center for learning.

In the British Isles, a child named Cuthbert was born who would become a light to many people in his lifetime. It is appropriate that his feast day is March 20, the first day of spring.

The Story of Cuthbert

Before sharing Cuthbert's story, explain to your students that we sometimes look at a photo album to remember or learn about someone. Although Cuthbert lived long before cameras and albums, children can imagine such an album for Cuthbert as they hear or read his story.

Assign eight readers beforehand and have them practice reading their "page." Also, ask them to illustrate their part of the story. If your class is large, invite children to take turns being readers and/or illustrators.

Narrator   I invite you now to look into an imaginary photo album where you will learn about a saint who lived a long, long time ago. His name is Cuthbert, and this is his story.

Reader 1   This is the first page of Cuthbert's photo album. Imagine a group of boys, about eight years old. They are playing, challenging each other to do handstands and cartwheels. Suddenly, a very small child, only three years old, comes running up, halting in front of a boy named Cuthbert. "Stop playing games!" the small child orders. Confused, Cuthbert stops to listen. The little boy goes on, "God wants you to teach other people someday. You should be home studying!" Cuthbert remembered this incident for a long time.

Reader 2   Now we see Cuthbert as a teenager. He is a shepherd, watching over a flock of sheep on a quiet, starless night. Cuthbert sees a beam of light in the sky streaming down to the earth, like a path. Angels begin moving on this path. They stop and pick someone up, a person who is glowing as brightly as the angels themselves. They carry this person upward, and then the sky is dark once more.

Some days later, Cuthbert learns that when he had the vision, the bishop, a very holy man, had died. Cuthbert decided the vision was God's way of telling him to join a monastery, to continue the work of the bishop. He returns the sheep he was tending to their owner, finds a horse, and sets off for a monastery.

Reader 3   As a monk, Cuthbert travels the countryside, teaching people about Jesus. Sometimes, it is said, he heals people. Picture now a frightened mother in a small village running up to Cuthbert. Her baby lies in her arms, so ill that he is near death. Gentle Cuthbert kisses the child. The baby opens his eyes, color returns to his cheeks, and he smiles. The grateful mother tells many people of the miracle in her arms.

Reader 4   Pretend you can see Cuthbert and a young boy walking along a river. They are hungry, so Cuthbert suggests they pray for food. From high in the sky, a magnificent eagle swoops down, plunges into the water, and emerges with a large salmon. The bird drops it near the boy. Gleefully, the child picks up the fish so Cuthbert can cook it. "Don't you think," says Cuthbert, "that we should give half of this to our kind fisherman?" So the eagle feasts that day, too.

Reader 5   Imagine Cuthbert walking down to the sea in the evening, with a monk secretly following him. All day Cuthbert has been teaching others about God, but he decides to give his night to God as well. The other monk watches from the shadows, curious about what Cuthbert is going to do, and he is amazed at what he sees.

Cuthbert walks into the sea, until the water reaches his chest. There he stands for hours, singing praises to God, until dawn streaks the eastern sky. Returning to the shore, Cuthbert kneels down, still praying. Two little sea otters tumble playfully out of the water. They scramble up to Cuthbert's very cold feet. They breathe their warm breath on his feet, and dry them with their sleek fur. Cuthbert blesses them, and they scurry back to the sea.

Reader 6   Cuthbert longs to live all by himself so he can devote all his time to God. Pretend you can see his lonely island of Farne; Cuthbert is digging a tiny two-room shelter there. Soon he learns, however, that he is not alone: many birds live there, too, and they destroy Cuthbert's garden and roof. One day, he sees two crows who are causing much damage. "Shoo! Go away!" Cuthbert commands.

The two birds leave, but as Cuthbert continues to work, one crow returns. Its head is bent down, its wings are actually drooping, and it croaks at Cuthbert, as if to ask his forgiveness. Cuthbert smiles and nods. The crow leaves, returns with the other crow, and they fly happily around Cuthbert. They live in peace from then on.

Reader 7   Cuthbert loves his little island and his time alone, but others often visit him. One day, the visitor is the king himself, asking Cuthbert to leave the island and become bishop. Cuthbert does not want to, but he believes that if God sent the king to his humble island, it must be God's plan for him to become a bishop. He begins a new life on the mainland.

Reader 8   Cuthbert is very old now. He has shown people God's love in many, many ways. Now he knows that he will die soon, and he longs to be with God. He goes back to his beloved island of Farne with a few of his monks. There he dies peacefully. Now imagine a large, sparkling light in the darkness; in order to give others on the mainland a sign of Cuthbert's death, the monks make a huge torch in the darkness on a high hill. They want all to see that the great light they knew as Cuthbert has gone to his God.

Narrator   We close our photo album now, but notice that the feast of Saint Cuthbert is March 20, the date of the spring or vernal equinox. On this day, day and night are each exactly twelve hours long. Cuthbert's life is like the equinox: he shows us that God's love is with us equally in times of darkness and light, in good times as well as bad.

Activities

1. Plan and stage a skit of Cuthbert's life, using ideas from the "photo album." Have children use the scenes from the preceding story, writing dialogue based on the text. This play could be given for other students, parents, or residents in a nursing home.

2. Make a multimedia mural showing God's love. Challenge the children's thinking abilities by encouraging the creation of a mural that is both concrete and symbolic, current and historical. For example, signs of God's love can be found in newspaper articles about someone helping someone else, in magazine articles on breakthroughs in medical research, or in pictures of modern-day peacemakers.

   Signs for the mural can also be made with Old Testament symbols, such as Jacob's ladder or Moses' burning bush. Hand and finger prints and baby pictures can be added, connecting God's people of long ago to God's people of today.

   Signs of spring—whether drawn onto the mural, made with textured fabrics and pasted on, or fastening the actual objects onto the mural—will add visual and textural interest. The final appearance of the mural, however, is less important than the making of it. The process will help children see that they can look at any topic from many angles, and that they have taken the most important topic and shown themselves how infinite are the ways in which God is revealed to us.

Timeline

Using the information at the beginning of this chapter and in the story, add the seventh-century segment to your timeline.

More Saints of This Century

Fiacre (born at the beginning of the century); Isidore of Seville (c. 560-636); Martin I (d. 655); Bathildis (d. 680); Bertilla of Chelles (c. 635-705).

Richard
Died 720

Winebald
Died 761

Walburga
Died 779

Willibald
Unknown

In the eighth century, a child named Bede was born in northern England. His life would be profoundly affected by the presence of a monastery set along the nearby Tyne River.

When he was six years old, he began his education with the monks there, and spent his entire adulthood in that monastery, studying, teaching, and writing. Gathered in this monastery were books from all over Europe, and Bede's life work centered on these. One of his writings was the *Life of Cuthbert*. His *History of the English Church and People* earned him the title "Father of English History." He was seen as the most learned man of his time.

During Saint Bede's quiet but illustrious (and industrious) lifetime, lived another saint whose life was a sharp contrast to Bede's. His name was Boniface, and he too was an English monk. But unlike Bede, he was to travel far and live a rugged life, and baptize thousands of people. After working in his native England, he moved to what we call the Netherlands, and then to Germany, where his missionary work was so extraordinary, he became known as the "Apostle of Germany."

One of Boniface's supporters was Charles Martel, leader of the Franks, a group of people originating in what is now northern Germany. Martel believed that Christianity would unite other northern tribes and the Franks. Charles was succeeded by his son, Pepin the Short. After ten years with the title of "mayor," Pepin decided he was doing the work of a king and deserved to be called one. The current pope, Zachary, approved, for he understood that the Church in the West could no longer depend on the emperor of the East. Now the pope had another civil power to turn to if necessary. In 751, acting as the pope's legate, Boniface crowned Pepin king of the Franks. This made the king of the Franks obligated to the pope, and it meant the Church in Rome no longer needed the East for protection.

Boniface's accomplishments were staggering in terms of numbers of converts, but the act of crowning Pepin had its own far-reaching effects. When the pope was threatened in Italy by the Lombards and received little help from the Emperor in the East, he turned to Pepin. Pepin came through the Alps to drive off the Lombards. Then he gave a part of Italy to the pope, land which became known as the Papal States. This put the pope in the position of a ruler or king. No longer was he a spiritual leader only, but he was a landholder, vulnerable to attack or political controversy as any other king. This situation would last for more than eleven hundred years.

Pepin's successor was his son Charles, who became known as Charlemagne, meaning "Charles the Great." His conquering zeal brought many into the Catholic Church. His great influence would continue into the early years of the next century.

Part of Boniface's work was to recruit others to help spread Christianity. Among his recruits were two brothers and their sister. Some say that Saints Winebald, Willibald, and Walburga were nephews and niece of Boniface. In any case, it is known that the support they offered each other enabled them to contribute greatly to Christianity in Germany. Walburga's feast day is February 25, though it is sometimes listed as April 30. Winebald's is December 18. (There is no known record of the dates of Willibald's birth and death.) Their father, Richard, also a saint, is remembered on February 7.

A Family of Saints

This family of saints teaches us how the encouragement family members receive from each other can heavily influence life choices and accomplishments. Before telling this story, give each child a piece of drawing paper and crayons or markers. Have the children divide the paper into four equal sections. As they listen to the story, have them draw scenes from the story, one for each family member. Older children can be encouraged to use colors and patterns to symbolize the characters.

NARRATOR

In the eighth century, a family of saints-to-be flourished in the Christian community of Wessex in England.

The father was named Richard. He had two sons, Winebald and Willibald, and a daughter, Walburga. Richard was a nobleman, and he was a holy man who raised his children to hunger for God's love. He helped them see how they could use their talents to do God's work. When his children were adults, Richard and his sons decided to make a pilgrimage, or journey, to the Holy Land. Richard only reached Italy, and died there in the autumn of the year 720. He did not know then that his children would eventually be known for their work in teaching others about Jesus.

Willibald entered the priesthood. Perhaps he studied in Rome. When Willibald later became a bishop, he would have an important job for his brother.

Winebald remained in Rome to study after Richard's death. Then, he traveled back to England, to see his sister, Walburga.

Walburga had been educated in the convent of Wimborne in England, and later entered the order there. Like many English nuns of her time, she was a talented person who believed strongly in education for girls. Among her many duties was the study and the practice of medicine. She was known for her ability to cure diseases. When Winebald came back to see her, they decided that Walburga would travel to Rome with him.

When they were in Rome, the great Saint Boniface arrived there. He was working to bring Christianity to parts of Europe that we call Germany and France, and he needed well-educated people to help him. Boniface ordained Winebald as a priest, and then convinced Winebald to do mission work with him in Germany. Bishop

Willibald had a specific job for his brother in Germany: to start a monastery for students, and for training new priests. Through this and other work, Winebald helped lay the beginnings of Christianity in France, the Netherlands, Austria, Belgium, and Luxembourg, as well as Germany.

Boniface had plans for Walburga, too. She traveled with a group of sisters to Germany to help start a monastery there. Two years later, her brother Winebald began a double monastery. There was a section for women and one for men at a place called Heidenheim. Walburga joined him there, and she was abbess, he abbot. In addition to her work as leader of the women, she practiced medicine. Some years later, Winebald died, and Walburga became abbess for the whole monastery, until her death eighteen years later.

Saint Richard's family is remembered for all that they did to help spread Christianity during the eighth century. But they teach us something, too. Like your drawing in four sections, a family is made up of separate people, who can come together to encourage one another, and to help each other listen for God's call. Willibald encouraged his brother when he asked him to start a school. Winebald traveled the long way back to England to get Walburga, and later, they worked together. All of their work was for Jesus, whom they had learned about because of their father.

Activities

1. Talk with the children about how important it is for family and friends to encourage one another. Discuss what the siblings in the story did to challenge and support each other. Ask children to think about the people most important to them. Do they ever talk with these people about their talents, and about how they are following God's plan for their lives? Suggest some ways they might begin a discussion about this.

2. A good symbol for the kind of healthy family interaction shown in Richard's family is a patchwork quilt. It is many pieces coming together to form a useful, beautiful blanket. Separately, the pieces are small, but together they create something that is warm and strong as well as a work of art.

   Help children create their own family "quilts." Give each child a piece of burlap, perhaps a twelve inch square. Supply them with felt pieces in various colors, scissors that can cut felt, and glue. Quilts can be created by choosing colors that symbolize different family members, and piecing these together onto the burlap with glue. Older children may want to create designs with the felt, or they can use other fabrics with patterns. When the glue is dry, the quilts can be taken home as discussion starters on how families can support each other in doing God's work in the world.

Timeline

Using the information at the beginning of this chapter and in the story, add the eighth-century segment to your timeline.

More Saints of This Century

Bede (c. 672-735); Boniface (c. 672-754); John Damascene (c. 676-c. 749).

Notker Balbulus

Died 912

Tutilo

Died 915

For a few hundred years now, people in Europe lived amid great conflict as the order and structure of the Roman Empire disappeared and warriors looking for new places to settle conquered lands and peoples. There was a desire on the part of many of the Barbarians, however, to take on Roman ways. As a result, many converted to Christianity, as can be seen in the work of Saints Boniface, Walburga, Winebald, and others. But there was to be one more major invasion as the ninth century dawned. These invaders were called the Vikings.

From the cold lands of Scandinavia, the Vikings, or "sea rovers," were seafarers of remarkable skill. Their vessels, called longships, were made of overlapping planks of wood, which were light and could travel far, fast, and inland onto rivers. Sometimes they traveled for trade, venturing into Russia and as far away as the Mediterranean. Courageous explorers, they sailed to Iceland, Greenland, and even Newfoundland in North America.

Other times, they went in search of lands to settle. Fierce warriors, they struck terror into the hearts of those who lived in coastal settlements. Their actions were often like those of brutal pirates. Eventually they settled in some of the places they had raided, and founded great cities such as Dublin and Kiev. Many would become Christians. At this time, however, their arrival was terrifying for those in western Europe, and their presence would be a factor in the beginnings of the feudal system.

As the Vikings were roving far from home, the Chinese conquered Tibet. For five years in China there was a persecution of all religions but Buddhism. In 850, the first book was printed there.

While Roman architecture was crumbling, Europeans were replacing it with crude buildings. Roman roads and aqueducts fell into disrepair as knowledge of how to build them was forgotten. At this time, the Muslims were creating great architecture. Mamum the

Great ruled in Baghdad from 813-833, his rule marked by liberal religious attitudes and great artistic achievements. But in the opening year of this century, Catholic Church history would be forever changed by what must have appeared at the time to be a whimsical action of the pope.

It was Christmas Day, in the year 800, and Saint Peter's Basilica in Rome was filled with worshipers. It was cold. Even the rich, clad in fur-lined cloaks, were shivering, and the huge stone block walls oozed cold moisture. Among the crowd was a group of Frankish nobles. They had arrived a month earlier to defend Pope Leo III from rebellious Romans. Rumor had it that the grateful pope would reward their king, Charlemagne, in some way.

Charlemagne came into the Basilica on that Christmas Day, knelt down before the tomb of Saint Peter, and began to pray. As he finished his prayer and was about to stand up again, Pope Leo came up behind him, placed a crown upon Charlemagne's head, and bowed to him as one bows only to an emperor. Charlemagne was now officially the Holy Roman Emperor. The Roman Catholics in the church shouted out their approval, but Charlemagne himself was annoyed. He did not mind being called an emperor, of course, but this meant he was beholden to the pope. If the pope could crown him, the pope could take away the crown. Their two powers were officially united now, but the pope would have the last word in any conflicts. Charlemagne's crowning is said to be one of the most significant events of the Middle Ages in Europe.

It signified not only the rebirth of the old Roman Empire in the West, but the birth of a Christian one. By the twelfth century, it would be called the Holy Roman Empire. The pope wasted no time in literally putting on the appearance of an emperor himself, wearing imperial scarlet for the first time. His own Church officials assumed titles linked with royal offices. There were those who lamented that this imperial Rome was a far cry from the Rome of the apostles.

Charlemagne was an ambitious and religious man. He was determined to unite vast lands and Christianize them, and many non-Christians died as a result. But he also fostered good governing policies, and he was very interested in education. For the past several centuries, after the Roman Empire collapsed in the West, the great writings, music, and other arts established in the hundreds of years prior to the Middle Ages were in great danger of disappearing altogether in the chaos of the Barbarian invasions. If it had not been for the tremendous efforts on the part of those living in monasteries and abbeys, all this would have been lost.

Charlemagne's interest in education furthered these efforts. He invited scholars from all over Europe to his court, educating his own children as well as other worthy students who could not afford school. He issued standards for the education of clergy, and encouraged monks to set up schools and libraries if they had not already done so.

It is to these industrious people that we turn for this story. Among them are two lesser-known saints, Tutilo and Blessed Notker Balbulus, Irish monks who settled in Switzerland, in the monastery of Saint Gall, one of the most influential monasteries of the Middle Ages, a center of music, art, and learning throughout that time. Tutilo's feast day is March 28; Notker's is April 6.

The Story of Notker Balbulus & Tutilo

This story is told by an observer of Tutilo and Notker, so one reader will be needed. A chorus response uses Gregorian chant, with both Latin and English texts. The melody given here is simple to sing. To start, find a tone and hold that note through the first three syllables; move one note down on the fourth syllable, then back up. For the second phrase, stay on the tone for four syllables, move one note up on the fifth syllable, then back down. Practice singing these lines with the children before reading the story, and briefly tell them that the saints in the story wrote music like this.

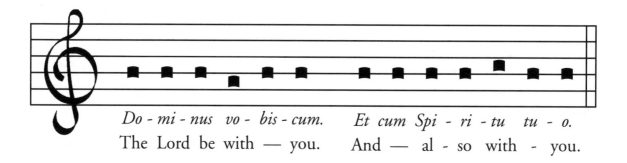

Do - mi - nus vo - bis - cum.   Et cum Spi - ri - tu tu - o.
The Lord be with — you.   And — al - so with - you.

Narrator   I am a monk at a monastery nestled among these vast and majestic mountains of the Frankish Empire. The monastery is called Saint Gall's because it was built over the place of that saint's tomb. Saint Gall died about two hundred years ago. Yesterday, some travelers arrived, all Irish monks. The spokesman for them is named Moengul, the others, Tutilo, Radpert, and Notker, being younger than he. They were in Rome; but instead of returning to their homeland, they will stay with us.

I find the one called Tutilo interesting. He will make a good addition to the community here, I think. I sense that he is intelligent and well-spoken. And no one will deny that he is very handsome. His sense of humor draws many to him, also. On the other hand, I am less impressed with his friend, Notker Balbulus. His name means "Notker the Stutterer," and it is too true that the man has great difficulty speaking. He is also weak of body. One wonders just how he could have traveled so far. But I must try to welcome him as well, as Jesus would. I wonder how they will settle into life here.

| **Chorus** | *Do-mi-nus vo-bis-cum. Et cum spi-ri-tu tu-o.* |
| | The Lord be with you. And also with you. |

| **Narrator** | The Irish travelers have brought much to our community here. Moengul has been appointed teacher to the younger monks, including Tutilo and Notker Balbulus, and they have proven to be worthy students. I am quite amazed at Tutilo's talents. He will become an exceptional musician, I think. He can also paint and sculpt beautifully. And of course, everyone enjoys his quick wit. But he is also a dedicated monk. I greatly admire him. |

Notker is a more able person than I thought when I first laid eyes on him. Clearly, despite his difficulties with speech, he is an excellent student. He, too, has musical talent. They are happy additions to the monastery of Saint Gall.

| **Chorus** | *Do-mi-nus vo-bis-cum. Et cum spi-ri-tu tu-o.* |
| | The Lord be with you. And also with you. |

| **Narrator** | As time goes on, I become more impressed with the monk named Tutilo. He shares his talents in numerous ways. It is not an exaggeration to say that he is a very capable musician, poet, painter, sculptor, builder, goldsmith, and composer! Much of the singing we do during prayer times, song called Gregorian chant, is written by Tutilo. For all his talents and good looks, he is not a proud man. No, he is living with his gaze fixed on God's great love. |

Now I have a confession to make. I was dazzled at first by Tutilo, and that kept me from appreciating Notker Balbulus. What a blessed man he is! His speech problems amount to nothing in the shadow of his holiness and his compassion for others. I am drawn to his warmth, as are the other monks. We enjoy the lively tone he sets here, and his wit brings laughter to many. He contributes to the music being written here, as well; his hymns are like music of the angels. Notker has other demanding duties, too: he is librarian and guestmaster, and one of the best chantmasters we have. How could I have ever looked at his frail body and thought that made him a weak man?

Chorus   *Do-mi-nus vo-bis-cum. Et cum spi-ri-tu tu-o.*
               The Lord be with you. And also with you.

Narrator   Our monastery has become known as a center for music, art, and learn-
               ing, and I feel much of this honor is due to our fellow monks, Tutilo
               and Notker. We supply all the other monasteries with our illuminated
               manuscripts of Gregorian chant. Those are truly works of art, and are
               greatly influenced by the talents of Tutilo and Notker. Tutilo is now
               head of the monastic school, so he touches the lives of many others
               through that, also. And Notker? Why, the other day, who should come
               to him for advice but the Emperor Charles!

               Notker has another talent, too. He is a writer. Recently he finished
               writing *Gesta Caroli Magni,* a book of folktales and legends of the great
               Emperor Charlemagne. These are becoming very popular stories!

               I am honored to know such talented men, but I am also grateful for
               their presence as holy men. Both are inspirations to me.

Chorus   *Do-mi-nus vo-bis-cum. Et cum spi-ri-tu tu-o.*
               The Lord be with you. And also with you.

Narrator   Alas, death takes from us those we love. A few days ago, our dear Notker
               left us. As much as we believe in his happiness in the afterlife, we are
               grieved for ourselves. This place will not be the same without our lively,
               spirited Notker. When we speak of him, each of us has tears in our eyes.

               Tutilo too is old now, as I am. I think back on the young Irish monks
               who came here long ago, and how they have enriched the Monastery of
               Saint Gall. I have known them as friends and as heroes. They were holy
               men. Perhaps some day they will be called saints. Both were greatly gift-
               ed by God, and their talents were immense. But they shared those tal-
               ents with the world.

               Sometimes, I think, God gives humans the ability to create beauty, so
               God's spirit can be spread and his love known to others through that
               beauty. I have no doubt that through Notker and Tutilo, many will
               come to know God.

Chorus   *Do-mi-nus vo-bis-cum. Et cum spi-ri-tu tu-o.*
               The Lord be with you. And also with you.

Activities

The role that monasticism played in European civilization is a fascinating one. Monasticism plays a significant part in our Church history, as well.

1. Look for books on the Middle Ages, especially children's nonfiction books, which show diagrams of the layout of monastery buildings and grounds. These will show how the monks were leaders and teachers in agriculture, practitioners of medicine, and providers of medical care as well as hospitality for travelers, and great educators. Encourage children to draw pictures of scenes they can imagine from a day in a monastery or convent, choosing one of the above areas.

2. Listen to recordings of Gregorian chant. Look for books that illustrate chant, and make copies of this writing to share with the children. Here is some background information on this important music.
   • It is the liturgical music of the Roman Catholic Church.
   • The chant is sung without the accompaniment of any musical instruments.
   • Originally, it was drawn from Greek, Roman, and Hebrew sources, which were part of Christian services from the very beginnings of Christianity.
   • It is named for Saint Gregory the Great, pope from 590-604, time period when chant was first collected.
   • It is also called *musica plana*, or plainsong. In later centuries, monks composed new variations that were more complex.

Timeline

Using the information at the beginning of this chapter and in the story, add the ninth-century segment to your timeline.

More Saints of This Century

William of Gellone (d. 812); Blessed Rabanus Maurus (784-c. 847); Methodius (c. 815-884); Cyril (826-869); Methodius of Constantinople (d. 847); and Edmund the Martyr (d. 866).

Wenceslaus

Circa 907-c. 935

In Persia in the year 900, a prince lay ill, but he was in capable hands. The physician worked quickly and efficiently. The prince's family marveled at this doctor, for he was barely out of his teens. Avicenna, the young Islamic physician, already had an excellent reputation.

As the century progressed, so did this remarkable young man. He served as chief minister as well as personal physician to rulers of Persia. These duties did not stop him from writing over one hundred books on a wide range of topics: poetry, medicine, philosophy, music, and astronomy. Reflecting the teachings of Aristotle and Plato, many of these would influence Christian scholars in the later Middle Ages. His major work, *Canon of Medicine*, would remain the leading medical textbook among Muslims and Christians for about six hundred years. At this time too, wonderful stories emerged from his culture that are still read today, stories called *A Thousand and One Nights*.

Far to the north, a little girl in Norway pulled off ice skates with animal bone blades and headed for the long farmhouse she called home. There was one main room in her house, where the family cooked, ate, and slept. Her favorite food, a meat stew, was simmering in a huge iron caldron on a tripod over the fire. When the day's work was done, she hoped to play "Hneftafl," a chess-like game, and to listen to her uncle spin exciting stories called sagas, about brave heroes.

Across the Atlantic Ocean, a great civilization began to decline. The Mayans started to abandon their palaces and religious centers. Why they did so remains a mystery.

In China, Prime Minister Wang Tan was grieving the death of his eldest son from smallpox. Fearing he would lose his other children to it, he called in the wise men and physicians of his country to find a possible remedy. There was one: a Taoist monk arrived in the capital with a technique called vaccination. This was eight hundred years before the same technique would be discovered in Europe.

During this century, the country of Ghana stretched to its greatest extent, from the Atlantic coast in the west to Timbuktu in the east. It was known as the "Land of Gold," but also had a large salt trade, and drew copper from the Sahara. These resources resulted in much wealth, and Ghana supported a large, well-equipped army. Its rulers became known for their wealth and lavish feasts. The capital was the city of Kumbi Saleh, one of the largest cities anywhere at that time.

The Christian Church continued to unfold in many ways. In the churches, a practice began of hanging a large cloth between the people and the altar at the beginning of Lent, hiding the heavenly glory symbolized by statues of saints and crosses of the risen Christ.

Politically, communications between the Eastern and Western Churches were alternately strained and friendly, and of course, always hampered by the slow course of travel. Both rulers in the East and West treated the Church as a department of their governments. This affected many aspects of the religion, including what was taught as part of the Christian message. In the West, civil rulers often chose the bishops, and bishops served as government officials since they controlled church-owned lands.

After Charlemagne's death, his great empire was eventually divided, with the inevitable fighting over land and power. Local lords were gaining power, castles were springing up in defense against the Vikings and other invaders. In eastern Europe, the Slavs, ancestors of today's Czechs, Slovaks, Croatians, Serbians, Bulgarians, Poles, and Russians, were farmers, hunters, and fishermen, little skilled at warfare.

In the ninth century, a Slavic state called Greater Moravia developed, and missionaries arrived. The first to come were from the Latin Church of western Europe. These German speaking missionaries made little progress without knowledge of the Slavic language. The Duke of Greater Moravia wanted greater political and religious freedom from the West, and so appealed to the emperor of the Eastern empire to help. The emperor responded by sending two Greek brothers who had spoken the Slavic language as children. The brothers were now both monks—Cyril, a professor, and Methodius, an abbot of a monastery for a time.

The emperor sent the brothers to the Slavic people, where they began a remarkable mission. They created an alphabet for the Slavic language, translated the Gospels and other sacred books into that language, and composed Slavonic liturgical books. They trained disciples and celebrated liturgies in the Slavonic language. This sparked a controversy among missionaries in the West, who claimed that liturgies should be celebrated only in Latin or Greek. Despite these conflicts, the brothers accomplished a tremendous amount, earning for themselves the title, "Apostles of the Slavic Peoples." Their work was accomplished in the later part of the ninth century.

Early in the tenth century, a child was born near Prague, the oldest son of Ratislav, ruler of Bohemia. His grandmother was Saint Ludmilla, wife of the first Christian duke of Bohemia. The child, Wenceslaus, was destined to become a saint himself, and patron saint of Bohemia, which is the modern-day Czech Republic. Some sources say Wenceslaus was a duke, and others, like the Christmas carol about him, say he was a king. His feast day is September 28.

The Story of Wenceslaus

By the end of the tenth century, Wenceslaus' feast day was observed throughout Bohemia. The shrine at his tomb became a place of pilgrimage, and miracles happened there. Wenceslaus' story is told here by a mother and child on their way to this site. It may be read by two readers, one taking the paragraphs with the mother's dialogue, the other taking the child's.

A mother and her child walked down the streets of Prague on a September morning. "We have a long walk, Ludmilla, and I want to reach the shrine of Saint Wenceslaus by midday," said the mother, taking the child's hand.

"Why are we going today, Mama?" Ludmilla asked, skipping along. "Who built the shrine, Mama? Who was Saint Wenceslaus?"

Mama smiled. "So many questions, Ludmilla! Well, a child who lives here must know all about our saint. Before you were born—before I was born—there was a young prince named Wenceslaus. At that time, many of the people who lived here were Christians, like us, but just as many were not. Often times, the two groups fought. Even in Wenceslaus' family, there were arguments, for his mother, Drahomira, was against Christianity and his grandmother, Ludmilla, was a Christian."

"Mama, the grandmother has the same name as me!"

"Yes. I chose the name for you because that Ludmilla became a saint, too. I wanted you to be named for her."

The little girl smiled, and the mother went on, "Grandmother Ludmilla was determined about two things: that little Wenceslaus would be raised as a Christian, and someday be a good king. She saw that he was taught well. When he was just thirteen, his father, the king, was killed in a battle. Wenceslaus would be the next king, but as he was so young, his mother was given the power of the king. Drahomira soon began to have Christians jailed, and then she had Ludmilla killed. This so angered the Christians that they eventually forced her out of the country, and Wenceslaus, only twenty years old, became king.

"He was a good king. He was a new kind of leader, for he made all his decisions based on what he believed Jesus would want him to do. He forgave his mother, so she could come back home. He changed the laws that jailed Christians, and had churches built. He was fair to people, whether they were poor or rich. He gave money to the poor, and passed laws that would protect people. Those who were hungry, children without parents, prisoners unfairly jailed were all helped by Wenceslaus. He did what he thought was right, even if others disagreed with him. Wenceslaus prayed every day, too. Some say he himself even helped make the bread and the wine used for Eucharist, using wheat and grapes from his own lands."

"Soon I will receive the Eucharist, Mama!" Ludmilla said.

"Yes, because of Wenceslaus, our country is a safe place for Christians like you and me. But it was not a safe place for Wenceslaus. Even though many people loved him greatly, there were still those who hated his ways. They were especially angered when the king made peace with the Germans, who had been their longtime enemy. And there was one person who was very jealous of him. That was his younger brother, Boleslav. He wanted to be king, and he saw that the men who hated Wenceslaus' ways could help him.

"Boleslav invited his brother to come for a banquet to celebrate the feast day of Saints Cosmas and Damian. The next morning, Wenceslaus walked to church, and at the steps he met his brother. Wenceslaus greeted him lovingly, thanking Boleslav for his hospitality. Boleslav said, 'Yesterday I did my best to serve you fittingly, but today this must be my service to you.' Then, he struck Wenceslaus with his sword! The brothers began to struggle, and immediately, other men ran up and killed Wenceslaus. As he was dying, Wenceslaus said, 'May God forgive you, brother.'"

"He was a good king, Mama," said Ludmilla quietly.

"Yes, he did a tremendous amount in the few years he ruled as king, and so he is still greatly loved, years after his death. The shrine we will visit today was built by Boleslav, who later regretted what he had done. But more importantly, Wenceslaus was a good Christian. He did what Jesus asks of all Christians. Look up ahead, Ludmilla. See all the people? They, too, are coming to the shrine. Many believe that miracles are worked there. The story of his life is finished, but it seems Wenceslaus' work for his people goes on."

Activities

1. Such well-loved saints as Wenceslaus often have legends told about them. Some are factual, others are based on the kind of person the saint was. A good example of this is the Christmas carol, "Good King Wenceslaus." It was written in the 1800s by a learned English scholar and hymnologist named John Mason Neale. He knew a great deal about this saint, so to show the generous and loving nature of Wenceslaus, Neale created the story that unfolds in his song. The melody is based on an old Swedish folksong. There are several beautiful picture books that depict this song. With these, you can see the times in which Wenceslaus lived, learn the song, and discuss what events or facts from Wenceslaus' life inspired Neale to create this story.

2. Wenceslaus stood for Christian values in a time and place very hostile to Christianity. In more recent times, the Christians of the Czech Republic have been challenged also. Older children can be encouraged to research the history of Christianity there during and after Communist rule.

3. Wenceslaus is a good example of a person who worked for social justice. Help students contact local Catholic Charities or Catholic Welfare offices to learn about issues of social justice and the poor. Then help children contact their state government information offices to express their support for legislation providing more justice for the poor.

Timeline

Using the information at the beginning of this chapter and in the story, add the tenth-century segment to your timeline.

More Saints of This Century

Ludmilla; Romuald (c. 950-1027); Matilda (d.c. 965); Peter Orseolo (d. 987).

Margaret of Scotland

Circa 1046-1093

As the eleventh century unfolded, the Sung dynasty in China encouraged development of the arts and sciences. Paper was first produced, gunpowder came into use, a printing process was begun, and the magnetic compass was invented. Despite such advances, the social structure remained unchanged. The people adhered to the philosophy of Confucius (551-479 B.C.E.), which taught a strict social hierarchy, with those of inferior status owing loyalty and respect to their superiors.

Elsewhere, Ghana was at the height of its power, controlling ports on the Atlantic and trade routes across the Sahara. The Turks came into power in Asia Minor, ending Byzantine control there. From then on, the area would be known as Turkey. Muslim culture and technology continued to advance, and in areas where there was an exchange of ideas among Muslims, Christians, and Jews, a rich civilization bloomed.

The chaos in Europe caused by centuries of

invaders resulted in a new social system called feudalism. By the eleventh century, it was entrenched in Germany, England, France, Spain, and Italy. A similar system was in use in Japan at this time. Land wealth and status set the stage for feudalism. Kings gave land to powerful barons and lords in return for military service. They, in turn, would give land on a smaller scale to lesser nobles or knights who would be loyal to them, helping them defend these lands.

Below them in status were the freemen and serfs. Freemen owned some lands but still spent several days a week working for a lord. The serf worked the lands of the nobles and could expect protection from the nobles in times of invasion. For these "privileges," the peasants were required to give the lord certain amounts of time and produce. They had very few rights, and were often seen as property belonging to a given area of land. Serfs and their families lived in abject poverty.

Knights, the soldiers of the time, came from

noble families and trained for their role for years. They developed a code of conduct called chivalry which combined traits of a good soldier and Christian values—at least to some extent. The knight was expected to be a brave, polite, generous, and loyal soldier, and to defend his family's honor and protect noblewomen. Yet these expectations did not extend to people of a lower social status.

Many castles were built between 1050 and 1350 to protect the feudal lands. The first castles were fortresses only, built into steep hillsides or atop rocky cliffs, and were made of wood. When these proved too easy to torch, stone castles were built. Castles were uncomfortable places to live in, with large but cold rooms where a lord and his knights, as well as terrified local people, could stay during attacks. The storerooms were huge, for a castle needed to contain enough food and supplies for many people for months if there was a siege. The upper floors were reached only by ladder.

As time went on, more space was designed for the lord and his family, as well as space for servants. Rich tapestries were hung to shut out at least some of the drafts. The courtyards might contain orchards and fishponds as well as exercise yards. Primitive lavatories were part of the improvements, as well. Towns often sprang up near castles.

In the year 1000, books were so rare and valuable that many people in Europe had never even seen one. They used sundials to tell the time of day but most likely would not know the date or even the year.

During this time, Church history was filled with political intrigue. Under German King Otto I, the Holy Roman Empire was created, consisting of Germany and northern Italy. Much vying for power ensued. While the popes claimed complete spiritual authority over Christian Europe, the emperors claimed they should control the Church's activities within their boundaries. Some emperors wanted the right to elect bishops. Conflicts between the pope and German emperors continued through the second half of the century. Pope Gregory excommunicated Holy Roman Emperor Henry IV in 1077, pardoned him after Henry did penance and asked for forgiveness, then excommunicated him again for later disputes over who controlled the Church.

Danes, Saxons, and Normans fought over the throne of England. In 1013, the Danish king, Canute the Great, was successful in conquering all of England. The Saxon heir to the throne, a child named Edward, was sent to Hungary for safety. There he grew up, marrying into that royal family. Thirty years later, Canute died, and the Saxons were back in power.

Prince Edward returned to England at the invitation of his uncle, Edward the Confessor, who was in power. The prince brought with him his son, Edgar. The prince did not live long, however, and when Edward the Confessor died, England was once again vulnerable for a takeover. Edgar was not yet old enough to take the throne.

William, Duke of Normandy, invaded England in 1066, winning the Battle of Hastings and consequently the throne of England. So important was this battle that an account of it was recorded in words and pictures on the Bayeaux Tapestry, 230 feet of linen, embroidered with colored wools. From that time on, the histories of France and England would be linked together.

There was another link, that between England and Scotland, that gives us the story of a delightful saint, a young woman of gentle strength who was born in Hungary, educated in England, and became queen of Scotland. Her name is Margaret, and her feast day is November 16.

The Story of Margaret of Scotland

Margaret's story is one of strong faith and action resulting in great improvements for many people. It is also the story of a marriage, and how love and a shared faith between two people can transform many lives. Here, the story is told in short chapters which cover different times in Margaret's life. Choose two or more readers to take turns reading chapters aloud.

CHAPTER ONE

Margaret stood quietly looking at the countryside of Hungary where she had played and studied during all of her nine years, often with her brother Edgar and sister Christina. Tomorrow they would leave. Would she ever be back?

But what lay ahead was so exciting! She and her family would travel to England, and live in Westminster Palace, because her brother Edgar was to eventually become the king of England. Her father, an English prince, had been sent to Hungary as a child for safety when Danish King Canute had taken over England. Later her father married Agatha, the niece of Hungary's queen, and Margaret, Christina, and Edgar had been born. Margaret understood that life was uncertain for her family because of her father's royal background, but she believed that whatever happened, God watched over her. Recently King Canute died, and Margaret's great-uncle, Edward the Confessor, had become king. He had sent word to Margaret's family to come to England. Margaret began to run toward her house, to prepare for her new adventures.

CHAPTER TWO

Margaret looked up from her studies. Edgar sat near her, intent on his writing. The kindly priest who was their teacher, was working with Christina now. Soon it would be time to stop and pray. Margaret enjoyed the schedule of study and prayer that her days brought. She loved everything about learning and reading, and she loved God even more.

Though Margaret's father had died soon after they arrived in England, the family had settled into life at Westminster Palace. Her uncle the king was a good man, a wise and careful ruler, and Margaret's life was a happy one. She smiled at her brother and sister, then went back to her reading.

CHAPTER THREE

Margaret sat quietly, prayerbook in hand. All around her were sights and sounds of mourning, for good King Edward had died. She, too, was filled with sadness, but she knew she must put aside these feelings to make an important decision.

Edgar was to be the next king, but he was still not old enough to take on such responsibility. Margaret had heard rumors of an invasion led by a man named William of Normandy. If his army were to win, Edgar would be in great danger, for the conquerors would not want heirs to the throne around! Perhaps she and Christina were also in danger. Now that she was twenty-one years old, Margaret felt she must be the one to protect Edgar.

After more prayer, she stood ready with a plan. They would flee to Hungary, where Edgar would be safe, and she and Christina could go ahead with their plans to enter a convent. Now, she must make arrangements for a ship to leave immediately.

CHAPTER FOUR

Margaret prayed as the ship rolled and rocked. Both fear and water overwhelmed the passengers as a great storm raged, stirring up huge waves that battered and engulfed the ship. They had only been at sea for a short time, and were still in the English Channel when the storm began. If they survived, where would they end up? Certainly not in the safety of Hungary. Trembling, Margaret continued to pray.

CHAPTER FIVE

The storm forced the ship into the North Sea. At last the ship limped to safety in Scotland's Firth of Forth. Margaret breathed a prayer of thanksgiving, but Christina grasped her arm and pointed. Coming towards the shoreline was a large group of warriors! Margaret and the others were led by the soldiers to the castle of the king. There they faced King Malcolm, a fierce-looking man, who held their future in his hands. They waited.

"Welcome," he said warmly. "Your uncle, King Edward, once sheltered me when I was in trouble. I can now do the same for you." He then arranged for a party to celebrate their arrival.

CHAPTER SIX

The fierce-looking king with gruff manners had a tender heart. And soon, that tender heart went out to the gentle and pretty Margaret. King Malcolm asked her to marry him. Margaret, intent on entering a convent, refused. She continued to pray, and to observe the rough people and countryside of Scotland. She questioned the lack of learning and culture here. She saw Malcolm's temper, his crude manners, his struggle to rule. He was more of a soldier than a courtly king.

But Margaret saw, too, that beneath his coarse manner, Malcolm was a good man, and he loved Margaret dearly. She decided that God was calling her to marry Malcolm. Margaret stood beside Malcolm in the castle at Dunfermline, in the midst of a beautiful plain, surrounded by woods and a rocky river. There, at the age of twenty-four, she became his wife and Scotland's queen.

CHAPTER SEVEN

Not long after the wedding, Malcolm noticed that his bride left the castle at a certain time each day. One day, he followed her and discovered she was using a cave as a chapel. He sat quietly with her as she prayed. Then he asked her if he could make the cave into a proper chapel. "I know nothing of God, but I do know that I love you," he said.

Each day, they sat together in the chapel, Margaret praying and reading Scripture to Malcolm. He would take her prayerbook and kiss it from time to time. One day, Margaret could not find the prayerbook. Even as a queen, she owned only three or four books. How could she have lost something so precious to her? Then Malcolm came in, a smile on his face, hands behind his back. "Missing this?" he asked, grinning. Then he handed Margaret the prayerbook, now bound in gold and silver and dotted with jewels!

CHAPTER EIGHT

Their life together was like that prayerbook. Outwardly, it had a royal appearance, but inside there was holiness and love, held together by Scripture and prayer. Nourished by a structured spiritual life, Malcolm and Margaret cared for the people of Scotland. They held important religious meetings called synods so others would better understand Church rules. They had beautiful churches built. During Advent and Lent, two hundred hungry people were invited to come to the castle each night to eat. Malcolm went down one side of the hall, dishing out food, and Margaret served the people on the other side. In Lent, they would rise during the night to attend Mass, and often gave out food on their way. They also brought learned teachers and books to Scotland to encourage education. Through the influence of his beloved Margaret, Malcolm became a king known for his just and caring ways toward his subjects.

Margaret never sat to eat until she had seen that orphaned children were fed first. She often worked with sick people, and would give away her cloak if she saw someone who needed it. Soon it became a game among the knights who rode with her to give away their cloaks, too. The queen set up hostels for weary travelers. She organized women's groups for study, prayer, and embroidery, making vestments and linens for the churches. Some days, she sat on a large rock outside of the town to listen to poor people who came to tell her of injustices done to them. Like Jesus, everywhere she went, she was surrounded by needy people.

CHAPTER NINE

Margaret and Malcolm were blessed with two daughters and six sons. Margaret's affection for the people of Scotland was mirrored in her household. She prayed daily for her children, saw that they had excellent teachers, and frequently checked on the children's progress. She taught their religion classes herself. Though they were princes and princesses, Margaret encouraged them to discount riches, and instead to love God. As soon as they were old enough, her daughters went with her as she tended the poor and helped others. Margaret also encouraged the castle servants to study; they found their queen to be a sweet and tender teacher.

Margaret and Malcolm were married about twenty-four years when they both died within days of each other. Their children went on to become wise rulers too, but the country of Scotland would never forget its cherished queen who was brought to them through a storm at sea.

Activities

1. Margaret was a fortunate woman for her time: she had never experienced hunger, she was well-educated, she had a loving family, and probably had all the material things she needed in her life. In that sense, she was like many Americans today. She is recognized as a saint for the loving way in which she used her material gifts to serve others.

Explore with the children which gifts they have among those listed here: family, food, medical and dental care, shelter, clothing, education, books, friends, transportation, church and neighborhood communities, entertainment. Help them see these as blessings. Encourage them to ponder the Scripture passage: "Of everyone to whom much has been given, much will be required" (Lk 12:48). Brainstorm with the children about ways in which they can share the blessings they have received with others.

2. Margaret's uncle the king became Saint Edward the Confessor. Read about him and discuss why he is a saint.

3. Children are often fascinated with castles and knights. Bring in children's non-fiction books with plenty of pictures of castles and castle life. *A Medieval Castle* by Fiona MacDonald and Mark Bergin, is particularly helpful and includes a glossary of medieval words. Challenge children to find out what these words mean: coffyn, chute, jerkin, and scullion.

Timeline

Using the information at the beginning of this chapter and in the story, add the eleventh-century segment to your timeline.

More Saints of This Century

Peter Damian (1007-1072); Gregory VII (1020-1085); Stanislaus (1030-1079); Bruno (c. 1030-1101); Anselm (1033-1109); Edward the Confessor (d. 1065).

Isidore, the Farmer
1070-1120

In the twelfth century—as in every century—there were many people whose names will never be known to us. Take, for example, an anonymous girl—one of many like her—who might grow up to become an English noblewoman. In the quiet of her home, she would learn to fly a falcon, play chess, read and write Latin, draw, embroider, and run a large household. She would also learn how to prepare herbs and medicines, for there were few doctors, and the role of physician fell to the women of the household. This girl would be betrothed by age seven, and married by fourteen.

Yet also in the twelfth century, there lived people who have been remembered for centuries, such as Saint Bernard of Clairvaux. He became known as a leader within an order of monks called the Cistercians. Despite a desire for solitude and simplicity, he was often called upon by others because of his ability to settle disputes. A person of many talents, Bernard is sometimes called "The Man of the Twelfth Century," and was named a Doctor of the Church.

During the time Bernard was doing his work, Thomas Becket was enjoying a luxurious life using his considerable talents as chancellor for King Henry II of England. When Henry appointed Thomas archbishop of Canterbury, however, Thomas changed his lifestyle, living simply as a monk and working to protect the Church. Several years of conflicts followed as Thomas and Henry clashed over Henry's desire to control Church matters. Frustrated by Thomas' adherence to his conscience, Henry had Thomas murdered. Becket is considered the most famous martyr of the Middle Ages.

The pendulum of agreement and conflict swung back and forth. German princes were able to end the dispute between the emperor and the pope over appointments of bishops. In a move that was anything but peacemaking, however, the King of France, Philip II, banished Jews from France in 1182.

Perhaps the most striking examples of power in the twelfth century were two phenomena of the High Middle Ages: the crusades and the cathedrals. Both were expressions of faith, in vastly different ways.

Since the fourth century, Christians had been making journeys, called pilgrimages, to holy places such as the tombs of saints and the Holy Land. Muslims had taken over Jerusalem in 638, but did not stop Christian pilgrims from coming in. When the Turkish Muslims captured Jerusalem from the Arabs in 1076, however, they started turning Christians away, even arresting and torturing some of them.

The Emperor of the Eastern Roman Empire asked for help. And so, at the end of the eleventh century, Pope Urban II called for a crusade, that is, a "War of the Cross," in hopes of winning back the Holy Land. This first crusade was successful militarily as Jerusalem was eventually regained. But success was won at a horrible price. Christians fought each other at times; to gain Jerusalem, Christians massacred Jews and Muslims. Jews were slain along the way to the Holy Land, and in Jerusalem itself, they were burned in their synagogues.

By 1133, Saint Bernard and other preachers called for a second crusade. The kings of France and Germany responded, but this crusade failed calamitously. By 1187, all the lands taken in the first crusade were again under Muslim rule. A third crusade, under the direction of King Richard the Lion-Hearted of England, regained some land, but disease, infighting among the crusaders themselves, and battles caused devastating casualties.

Just a few years into the thirteenth century, Pope Innocent III called for a fourth crusade, but he was met with little support. The actions of the Roman soldiers he did manage to rally caused irrevocable damage to relations between the Greek, or eastern, Christians, and the Roman Christians when these soldiers ruthlessly vandalized the most beautiful Christian city in the world, Constantinople.

By the mid-thirteenth century, the spirit of the crusades was broken, the Holy Land remained under Muslim rule, and conflict between the Church in the east and west had worsened. The crusaders, however, learned much from this conflict with the more advanced Muslim culture. These discoveries would lead to the period of Western history known as the Renaissance.

The other great expression of faith, the building of the cathedrals, left a legacy which still graces Europe today. With no power tools or cranes, builders hoisted huge blocks of stone four hundred feet into the air, and then fit them together, creating beautiful, three-dimensional pictures. Craftsmen made stained glass windows, and statues were tucked in the many recesses on the walls.

Cathedrals took years to complete: the Notre Dame Cathedral was begun in 1163, and completed in 1253. They were meant to inspire people with the beauty of God, and be used as a space for public worship. Some saw them as signs of the privilege and wealth of a few, but in fact they did become centers for the community at large. Meetings were held in them, travelers slept in them, and plays were performed on the steps. For the many illiterate people, the cathedral was a visual religious education, with its carvings and windows depicting Bible stories.

In contrast to the power and violence of the crusades, and the grandeur and wealth of the cathedrals, is the story of Saint Isidore of Spain. His life was a constant expression of faith, but one lived in the poverty and humility of a peasant. His feast day is May 15.

The Story of Isidore the Farmer

Isidore's story begs to be illustrated. Choose three children (or form teams, if more are interested) to illustrate each one of the three anecdotes within this story. Use poster board so the illustrations can be held up and easily seen at the appropriate moments in the story. Then choose four readers.

Reader 1   Saint Isidore was born in the year 1070, to a poor family in Madrid, Spain. When he was barely big enough to carry a hoe, he began working for a wealthy landowner named Juan de Vergas, on whose land he would work all his life. Isidore married Maria Torribia, who is now known as Saint Maria de la Cabeza. They had one son, who died when he was very little.

Isidore and Maria did not have much in life, and it would seem they had little to hope for. Yet they found meaning in their hard lives by loving God and caring for others. Isidore prayed all day as he plowed. He often visited churches in Madrid on his day off, and he and Maria shared what little they had with others. Here are three stories that show how Isidore lived as Jesus taught, and how others came to see him as a saint.

Reader 2   One day, Isidore was walking down the road. At his church there was going to be a supper, and Isidore was looking forward to it. From the field near the road, a ragged-looking man approached Isidore. "Please, sir, do you have some food?" he asked.

Isidore smiled. Many hungry people came to him. He usually gave them what he had, but as he had nothing today, he said, "Come with me, my friend, to the church supper. There will be plenty to eat there!" The two walked down the road, talking, and did not notice the poor woman with three children standing near a tree until one of the children cried out, "We are hungry!"

"Come along!" Isidore invited, scooping up the youngest child.

As they walked along, more and more poor people joined them, and Isidore invited each one to the church supper. Quite a crowd arrived at the church for supper that evening, with Isidore in the lead.

"Isidore!" one of the women exclaimed. "Do you expect us to feed all these people? We don't have nearly enough food!"

Isidore smiled confidently at her. "These people are Christ's poor. He will provide for them," he said.

She frowned, but began handing out food. All those who had come before Isidore and all those with Isidore received plenty! The woman looked over the happy crowd, and then at Isidore. "This reminds me of the Bible story of the loaves and fishes," she marveled, and then got her own dinner.

Reader 3   It was a cold winter day when Isidore walked down the road, a bit hunched over because of a large sack of grain on his back. He was on his way to the mill to have the grain ground into flour for his master's family. From the trees up ahead came the sound of many birds. Isidore loved animals. He and Maria always treated them tenderly. Today, his heart went out to these little ones who sounded so very hungry. He stopped, let the bag slip from his back, and poured half of the grain onto the ground. Immediately, the crowd of birds flitted down to feast. Isidore was so intent on watching them, he did not hear the approach of some other workers also on their way to the mill.

"Wasting your master's good grain on some silly birds, Isidore?" one teased.

"I wonder what he'll say when that bag is weighed at the mill!" the other said.

"The birds are God's creatures, too," Isidore answered mildly, and slung the sack with the remaining grain onto his back.

All three men walked to the mill. When the bags were weighed, Isidore's bag was miraculously full again. The other two men looked at each other in wonder.

Reader 4   The sun was streaking the eastern sky when Juan de Vergas walked out toward his fields, a worried frown on his face. As the owner of a great deal of land, he had many people working for him, and Isidore and Maria were among his favorites. He felt they were somehow a blessing to his own family. When some other workers came to him, complaining that Isidore came late to the fields each morning, Juan was troubled. He did not want to find out that Isidore was not as good a man as Juan believed.

When he reached the fields, Juan saw his other workers hitching oxen up to their plows. Isidore was nowhere to be seen. Juan hopefully scanned the other fields and even the roads, but he did not see Isidore. As the sun rose higher, Isidore came walking down the road, on his way back from church. He did not see his master, and immediately went to work behind his oxen.

Isidore worked steadily, praying as he went along row after row. Juan could see that Isidore loved working the earth. He would stop to examine a clump of plants, touching them gently, patting the warm soil around them. Still, Juan had to admit that Isidore was late. Unhappily, he was about to call to him when he saw two other men now working alongside Isidore. Confused, Juan looked around. Where had they come from? Who were they? Isidore seemed unaware of them. And, they each drove pure white oxen!

"Isidore!" Juan called. "Who are these other men helping you?"

Isidore looked up, noticing his master for the first time. Then he looked around him, seeing nothing. "What men, sir? I do not ask for anyone's help but God's."

Isidore stood looking at Juan with his open, honest face. Juan suddenly realized the other men were gone, as mysteriously as they had come. But half the field was plowed now. Juan's heart pounded. Isidore's helpers were angels!

"Did you want something, sir?" Isidore asked.

"Oh, I...." mumbled Juan, still stunned. Then happily, he added, "I just wanted to say may God be with you, Isidore."

Isidore smiled broadly, and went back to his plow.

Activities

1. In the United States, Isidore is the patron of the National Rural Life Conference, and some dioceses have prayer services and festivals for his feast day. If feasible, contact your diocesan Rural Life office and inquire about various activities. Inform the children of these, and point out that Isidore would never have imagined that these activities would be carried out in his honor. Our actions can also have repercussions that we might never know about, for good or for ill. Discuss how our actions might affect others, as well as ways we can become more aware of the effect of our actions on others for the good.

2. Plant something in honor of Isidore. It could be a flowering bush outside of a nursing home, or a bean seed in a cup. Talk about the importance of soil. Make a connection between our food and soil by listing different types of foods and how they are produced. Highly processed foods such as pizza would be a good challenge for older children: where do the ingredients for the crust come from, and the cheese, the herbs, the tomato sauce, and pepperoni? Help them see that all food, even that from animals, originally comes from the soil.

3. Consider bringing in the book, *Cathedral, The Story of Its Construction,* by David Macaulay, to share with the children. It is an excellent companion to this chapter's cathedral section. With illustrations on each page, it takes readers through the entire, amazing process of building a Gothic cathedral. When readers are finished with the book, they will have a feel for the ingenuity and skill it took to build a cathedral, as well as for the numbers of people involved in the process.

Timeline

Using the information at the beginning of this chapter and in the story, add the twelfth-century segment to your timeline.

More Saints of This Century

Norbert (c. 1080-1134); Bernard (1090-1153); Hildegard of Bingen (1098-1179); Thomas Becket (1118-1176).

Hedwig
1174-1243

In the thirteenth century, a small, holy man in a brown robe was preaching and challenging the status quo in Italy. Francis of Assisi started his Order of Friars Minor around 1210. Long before the century was half over, this humble order grew to thousands of monks. Similarly, his friend Clare lived her life of extraordinary holiness in poverty, and her legacy to the world was the order of Poor Clares.

Francis the peacemaker had a powerful spiritual effect on the people of Italy. Meanwhile, England took a giant step toward a peaceful society with political resolutions. On the banks of the River Thames, the Magna Carta was signed, guaranteeing justice and fairness in tax collection and imprisonment.

While in France, Dominic, a Spanish priest, founded the Order of Preachers. The Dominicans, as they came to be called, soon established themselves in major university centers of Europe. Among their professors was a priest named Thomas Aquinas. Education flourished in many places, with the founding of the universities of Cambridge and the Sorbonne. An English philosopher and scientist at Oxford University, Roger Bacon, proved that eyesight could be improved with the use of lenses.

Science and mathematics made other advances. The Chinese introduced papermaking and gunpowder to Europeans. Mathematicians in Europe were replacing Roman numerals with Arabic ones, and also learned new mathematical concepts such as fractions from the Arabs. Road travel was improving in parts of Asia and Europe; in the Americas, the Incas were coming into power.

All was not peaceful, of course. Numerous crusades and wars raged throughout this century. Weapons were fierce: the battle ax, war hammers, and the double-edged sword. The Mongols emerged from China, under the leadership of Genghis Khan, to invade new territories. Their attacks were carried out silently, so only the sound of the horses' thundering hoofs could be heard, an eerie sound that struck terror in the hearts of those soon to be conquered.

Poland and numerous other countries endured these attacks. Christians in Europe, fighting among themselves, saw the Mongols as the punishing rod of God. Still, the Mongols brought improvements to their newly acquired empire, aiding orphans, building hospitals, and showing much religious tolerance. Marco Polo and his family traveled thousands of miles over mountains, deserts, and plains to reach China. When he returned, Polo published a book about the marvels he had seen. Many of the Europeans who read it, however, did not believe his reports.

Within the Church, conflict and glory played significant parts. Pope Innocent III had confrontations with England's ruler, John. Later, war broke out between Frederick II, who had led the sixth crusade, and papal allies. France's King Louis, a wise leader who had great compassion for his people, was can-onized by the end of the century. Scientist Roger Bacon was commissioned by his friend Pope Clement IV to write a compendium of all branches of knowledge: nine years later Bacon found himself imprisoned by the Church for heresy. From 1268 to 1271, there was no pope in power.

But most people led less colorful lives, working the land to stay alive. The peasants ate rye bread and leek soup, while the nobles dined on gingerbread. For those with the leisure to worry about it, it was considered bad manners to wipe your mouth on a tablecloth or to dip your fingers into a drink.

Amid its advances and conflicts, the thirteenth century was graced by the presence of a woman named Hedwig. Born into the affluence of Bavarian royalty, Hedwig was well-educated. Married to a Polish duke, she spent her adult life as a duchess in Poland. However, Hedwig saw her privileges not as a right but as a responsibility. She believed that she should use her good fortune to help others, and her consequent lifestyle and works made her a saint.

The Story of Hedwig

Introduce Hedwig with this simple play, told from three perspectives. Four readers will be needed: a narrator who speaks in the present time, two women of Hedwig's social status and time, referred to as Lady 1 and Lady 2, and Duke Henry, Hedwig's husband. Position the narrator in the middle, the two ladies on one side, the duke on the other.

Narrator   October 16th is the feast day of Saint Hedwig. She was born long ago, in the year 1173, at Castle Andechs in Bavaria. Her father was a count, a wealthy man with much power. When she married Duke Henry I of Poland, Hedwig became a Duchess, a woman of wealth and leisure time, for she had many servants to do her work.

Lady 1   Did you hear? The duke has married! The bride is named Hedwig, and she is the daughter of Count Berthold IV of Bavaria.

Lady 2   Yes, I've met her. I found her to be a friendly young woman, very energetic. She studied at the Benedictine convent in Kitzingen. And, I do think she and the Duke are quite taken with each other!

Duke Henry   I am Duke Henry, and I am a very, very lucky man. My marriage to Hedwig was arranged by our families. We did not know each other. You can imagine, then, that I was quite nervous when I first met Hedwig, for if we did not go along well together, we might be unhappy for the rest of our lives! But God smiled upon us. We have been in love with each other since the very beginning. Hedwig is a wonder! She is quick to learn, quick to ask questions, quick to care about others.

Narrator   Because of Henry's position as duke, Hedwig was wealthy, but she was also able to see the poverty of the peasants who worked for wealthy people like herself. Their poor living conditions troubled her deeply. She had other interests as well, for Hedwig and Henry were blessed with a large family, and she was a devoted mother.

Lady 1   Did you hear? The Duchess Hedwig is expecting another baby.

Lady 2   Yes, she is a good mother. Still, she seems to find time to bring food to the peasants. I've heard she brings clothing and even medicine to some of them! I wonder how Henry feels about this?

Lady 1   Have you noticed how she dresses? Such plain clothing! You'd never know she was a duchess! Certainly she can afford better...sometimes she even goes barefoot!

Duke Henry   My dear Hedwig has just had our seventh child! Beautiful children— Henry, Conrad, Gertrude, and the rest. Hedwig is a loving mother! Still, she does much for others, too. She has organized all the duties in her life so she can be involved with the poor. I encourage her in this. Often, in the evenings, with the baby in her arms, she talks to me about her concerns. Our wealth, she says, does not excuse us from thinking of others. She dresses simply. One day, she even came home barefoot! She told me she met a woman along the way who had no shoes, so Hedwig promptly took hers off and gave them to the woman.

Narrator   Hedwig and Henry lived during a difficult time in Poland's history. Other countries tried to take it over; within the country itself, powerful dukes fought among themselves for more power. Whenever possible, Hedwig attempted to hold peace talks, something no woman was expected to do. When these efforts failed, she had to watch her beloved Henry go off to war.

Lady 1   Now I have heard it all! When Henry's land was invaded, Hedwig rode out with him and spoke with the challenger! Whatever possessed her to do such a foolish thing?

Lady 2   She's tired of this constant warring, I suppose. She did make peace between them, though. I can't imagine how she got them to listen to her!

Duke Henry   We are all weary of war here. Yet, each time it begins, I am astounded at Hedwig. She hates all this strife, and so insists on being part of any meetings that might prevent war. I don't know what amazes me more: her courage, her intelligence, or her ability to talk sense into these war-loving men! And when I was so badly injured, she never left my side. It must be her love of God that brings her through all the hard times. We pray together, and I have no doubt that God hears her prayers.

Narrator   Despite the time spent in wars, Henry and Hedwig did a great deal to better their country. They brought comfort and relief to many poor people, even building hospitals. They also founded several monasteries, which meant that learning and religious life enriched the whole area. Their daughter Gertrude eventually became abbess, or head, of the monastery of Trebnitz.

Lady 1   Have you seen the new monastery?

Lady 2   Yes, and it is magnificent! Good things will come from there, I'm sure. We must be very grateful to Duke Henry for his generosity. He is a man of high religious ideals.

Lady 1   Hedwig was very involved, I have no doubt. I hear she has already begun plans for another monastery elsewhere. Will that woman ever slow down? I can't help but admire her, and wonder if there is something I could be doing....

Duke Henry   The monastery at Trebnitz is a sight to behold! I truly feel God was with us as we worked to bring that about. It is no small thing to build a monastery, and we have Hedwig to thank for it. I remember the day she came to me with the idea. I was talking with our daughter, Gertrude, when Hedwig came in. She smiled at us and began talking in that way I know so well. A hospital had just been completed, what did she want now? A monastery! It seemed impossible, but now we have done it!

Narrator   Hedwig's life was filled with both happiness and sadness. Two of their sons fought over Henry's land, and despite Hedwig's efforts to settle this disagreement, one son left and died soon after. Some years later, Henry died, and another son died in battle. Hedwig never lost her faith, however. She spent the rest of her life living in the monastery at Trebnitz, dying at the age of 69, in 1243. Her influence, however, was felt long after her death. Hedwig was declared a saint in 1267.

Activities

1. Hedwig personally worked to ensure peace in her time. In the spirit of her peace-making efforts, locate a group or cause that promotes a more peaceful society or social justice in your community, in your country, or in the world at large. Write for information about this group or organization, and see how you and the children can become involved in its work.

2. Hedwig gave bread to the hungry, and she was said to go barefoot, even in the winter. Thus there is a custom of baking bread in the shape of a shoe on her feast day. Share a bread snack with children to commemorate Hedwig, perhaps bringing in a variety of breads. Talk about the importance of bread in the diets of many people throughout the centuries. Then discuss how there are people in our time of plenty who are hungry. Help them see different factors that lead to this situation, such as joblessness, racism, and lack of education. If your church has a food pantry, or there is a local food shelf, help children organize a food drive.

3. For a fascinating, amusing, and sometimes dismaying look into the life of a young noble girl toward the end of the thirteenth century, read *Catherine, Called Birdy*, by Karen Cushman, an award-winning novel for children, ages 8-12.

Timeline

Using the information at the beginning of this chapter and in the story, add the thirteenth-century segment to your timeline.

More Saints of This Century

Dominic (1170-1211); Francis (c. 1181-1226); Clare (1194-1253); Anthony of Padua (1195-1231); Albert the Great (1206-1280); Elizabeth of Hungary (1207-1231); Bonaventure (1221-1274); Thomas Aquinas (1225-1274); Louis (1226-1270).

Catherine of Siena
1347-1380

At a time when most people never traveled more than a few miles from the village of their birth, an Arab man named Ibn Battuta traveled over 75,000 miles in his lifetime. In 1333, he reached India and was fascinated by the efficient mail service. Runners were posted every third of a mile. In one hand, each runner carried a baton with bells on top, and the letters in the other. He would run as fast as he could to the next runner, the bells alerting the next man to be ready.

During the fourteenth century, the Chinese drove out all foreign rulers and established the Ming dynasty. They launched several exploratory voyages, sailing to Southeast Asia, India, and East Africa. At this point in time, they were probably the most technologically advanced civilization in the world.

In Europe, the population had grown steadily, and the simple farm techniques in use could not produce enough food. The early years of the century were part of a twenty-five year famine, when people ate wild rabbits, birds, dogs, cats, and even the dung of doves. Robberies increased and charity decreased.

While most people lived in the country, towns began springing up in this time. Few towns had more than two thousand inhabitants. These market towns grew up around monasteries or castles or near harbors. Many serfs chose to run away from the nobles who held power over them, hoping to avoid capture. After a year, they would be freemen.

The towns were noisy places. Town criers shouted news, carts and horses clattered down cobbled streets, peddlers advertised their wares, and bells rang to announce meetings, the start of the work day, and church services. They were dangerous places, too; police services were meager and thieves lurked in the unlit streets. Also, the dense sprawls of wooden houses were vulnerable to fires which could consume whole districts.

Towns were dirty, contaminated places, where people threw rubbish and excrement into streets and rivers. Other sanitation practices were poor, also. The cold and damp encouraged respiratory diseases. Pigs and rats, carriers of typhus, typhoid, and influenza, roamed the streets. Victims of leprosy begged for alms, sounding a warning rattle that they were approaching.

These difficulties were minor, however, compared with what was to arrive: the bubonic plague. The Black Death, as it was called, was brought to Italy and North Africa in 1347, most likely on merchant ships, through infested fleas living on rats. It spread at an astonishing rate, reaching the northern areas of Russia and Scandinavia within four years. Whole towns were wiped out. Cemeteries filled up, and in some places corpses were not buried because the gravediggers had died. No one was safe from contagion. The bubonic plague attacked individuals suddenly. Parts of the body would swell up, with black and white splotches forming on the skin. After about three days of agony, the victim died.

The Black Death peaked between 1348 and 1350. At least one-third of Europe's population died. Those who survived faced further problems. Food supplies were diminished by the lack of farmworkers; schools and universities closed; charitable services dried up; important crafts were lost as masters died without passing on knowledge; and critical but unwritten laws were forgotten. Fear ran rampant. There were violent uprisings of peasants and artisans against nobles. Jewish people were sometimes accused of having spread the disease and were killed. Some Christians lost faith and turned to Satanic cults. Others, called flagellants, scourged themselves in hopes of purging the sin that may have caused the plague.

Superstitions increased. Belief in witchcraft was widespread in the fourteenth, fifteenth, and sixteenth centuries in Europe. At least 300,000 people were accused of witchcraft and put to death. Many people believed that if they walked far enough, they would reach the edge of the world, where an endless waterfall flowed. Alchemists tried to make gold using mercury and lead. Hoping to conquer death, many people searched for an elixir of life.

When Pope Gregory XI died, he was succeeded by a French bishop who was a personal friend of the French king, Philip. This new pope decided to live in a French town called Avignon, in a castle. He changed some church laws which the king did not like, and appointed French cardinals. His successor moved the papal offices from Rome, making Avignon his permanent home. The popes elected after him continued to appoint French cardinals and to live in France. In all, seven French popes lived in Avignon between 1309-1377.

Christians all over Europe were concerned about this, for they believed that the pope, as successor to Saint Peter, should live in Rome. The English were especially worried that the French king had too much power over the Church. The Hundred Years War (1337-1453), a series of conflicts between England and France, was in full swing, and the English feared that French popes would persuade other Europeans to side with the French.

Saint Catherine of Siena lived during this turbulent time, and a great deal of her life's work revolved around the papal conflicts. Recognized as an uncommonly holy person when she was in her twenties, she was asked to mediate disputes between city-states. In 1376, she intervened with the city of Florence and the pope to settle a dispute. In a time when women had little status and very few rights, Catherine was sought out by nobles and generals for advice. Her feast day is April 29.

The Story of Catherine of Siena

In Catherine's time, most women did not learn to read or write. Despite her many duties in the convent, Catherine learned to read and, around age thirty, taught herself to write. Knowing this will help the children understand and appreciate Catherine's extraordinary accomplishments. Her story is told in three speaking parts, with a chorus.

Brother Thaddeus
I am a monk living in the city of Siena, one of the followers of the wise Catherine. She is remarkable for her holiness as well as for her wisdom, and thus has many followers. With the help of some other followers, I would like to tell you about her work, for we predict that someday Catherine will be a great saint. We feel honored to assist her in her work.

All
Catherine was strong and good, and Jesus made her a peacemaker.

Brother Callistus
Like most women of our time Catherine cannot write, so she dictates letters to us. These letters are sent to lords and other nobles who are fighting and have asked for her help in settling their conflicts. Sometimes Catherine goes to talk with people from both sides. Little by little, she helps them see ways to compromise, to work things out. We are always astonished.

All
Catherine was strong and good, and Jesus made her a peacemaker.

Brother Caedmon
We were never so astonished as we were a few months ago when Catherine asked us to write a letter to the pope! And this was no ordinary letter, asking for his blessing. Oh, no! Catherine was giving him advice in the form of a gift. You see, the popes have always lived in Rome. We consider it a holy city. But lately, there has been much strife between kings and the pope's officials, and the pope decided to move to a place in France called Avignon.

Catherine believes that it is God's will that the pope go back to Rome, and so she found a clever way of telling him so. She sent him candied orange peel as a Christmas gift, along with a letter that says, "The taste of this gift is at first bitter, then sweet. That is how it is when you do God's will."

All	Catherine was strong and good, and Jesus made her a peacemaker.
Brother Thaddeus	Will Catherine be successful with the pope? Perhaps. She is guided by Jesus, and is powerful because of her devotion to Christ. So why were we so surprised that she should write to the pope? She has been building up to this for a long time. All her life, actually.
	She is the youngest child—the twenty-fifth!—of Giacomo and Lapa Benincasa, prosperous wool dyers. As a child she was friendly and cheerful, but liked to spend time alone. When she was only six years old, she had a vision. She saw Jesus with the saints Peter, Paul, and John. She decided then and there that she belonged to Jesus and that she would spend her life serving him.
All	Catherine was strong and good, and Jesus made her a peacemaker.
Brother Callistus	Catherine's parents wanted her to marry a wealthy man, but she refused, saying she wanted to work for Christ. Fearful that they would pressure her more, she cut off her long hair. What a shock that was for her parents! At first they were angry with her; but one day, her father saw a dove above her head as she prayed. He took this as a sign that Catherine should follow a religious life. She joined the Dominicans, not going to the convent but living at home, wearing a habit. For three years she lived mostly in her room, praying and having many visions. Then she was ready to serve Jesus in the world.
All	Catherine was strong and good, and Jesus made her a peacemaker.
Brother Caedmon	Catherine has many followers: monks like myself, laywomen and men, and priests. She has such a spiritual way about her! I can only say that she is the holiest person I have ever known. It has been a privilege to help her in her work as peacemaker, helping the poor, visiting prisoners, and serving the sick and dying.
	As for the pope, Catherine will continue writing to him, I am sure. I keep my writing utensils ready and a traveling bag nearby. I will not be surprised if she decides to go to France, to meet with the pope himself; that's how greatly she desires peace in the Church.
All	Catherine was strong and good, and Jesus made her a peacemaker.

Activities

*To more fully understand the times in which Catherine lived, look for the book **The Door in the Wall**, by Marguerite de Angeli. De Angeli won the Newbery Medal for this title, as well as the Regina Medal from the Catholic Library Association. Set in fourteenth-century England, this story follows a boy of a noble family who plans to begin his education in the ways of knighthood, but becomes sick with an illness (perhaps polio) and loses the use of his legs. He is helped emotionally, physically, and spiritually by a group of monks.*

This book is particularly relevant to this chapter because it describes the different social classes, the horrors of the Black Death, the political climate, and the richness and challenges of life in a monastery.

1. Consider reading aloud parts of the book that particularly describe life in the fourteenth century.

2. The title of the book, *The Door in the Wall*, is taken from Scripture (Rev 3:8). The author uses the image of a door in the wall both realistically and symbolically. Challenge children to read the book and find the ways de Angeli uses them.

3. Help children research the nationalities of the popes over the past two hundred years.

Timeline

Using the information at the beginning of this chapter and in the story, add the fourteenth-century segment to your timeline.

More Saints of This Century

Elizabeth of Portugal (1271-1336); Julian of Norwich (d.c. 1423); Bridget of Sweden (c. 1303-1373); Sergius of Radonezh (1315-1392).

John of Kanty

1390-1473

In fifteenth-century Korea, King Taejong regretted that his son Sejong had been born third in the family line for the throne. His older sons were intelligent and respectful children, models of a Confucian society, but Taejong recognized a greatness in young Sejong. So did his brothers. The crown prince purposely disgraced himself, living a wild, unprincipled life long enough to be declared unfit for the throne. The second brother shocked his family by becoming a lowly Buddhist monk. Thus, the third son could become the wise and compassionate king his father had foreseen.

Under Sejong's rule, his country experienced the Golden Age of Korea, where the arts, sciences, and social welfare made tremendous leaps forward. His greatest accomplishment was the creation of a phonetically perfect alphabet. Sejong never forgot his brothers' unselfishness. Centuries later, the Korean people would still celebrate this king.

In Africa, the city of Timbuktu, wealthy because of its many resources, also became known as the "City of Scholars." Students went there from all over Africa. Rich and poor, they all studied. The poor students often supported themselves by working as tailors, and so tailors gradually became known as learned men.

As life was blossoming in Korea and parts of Africa, this springtime of sorts—when old ways were dying and giving life to new ways—was happening in Europe, too. This change was especially marked at mid-century: for example, a German diamond polisher named Johannes Gutenberg invented a method of printing using movable type. The Koreans and Chinese were already using this method of printing, but it was Gutenberg's efforts that profoundly affected Europe.

Now books could be produced much faster and more cheaply than ever before, enabling many people to own books, encouraging others to want to read, and spreading new scientific knowledge rapidly. The first book

Gutenberg printed was the Bible. Saint Augustine's *City of God* was also produced, with twenty-four editions printed in the 1400s. The feudal system was breaking down, the effects of the bubonic plague being one of the factors in its demise.

As a result of these changes in the social system, independent city-states formed in Italy. In these there was a renewed interest in learning and art, marking the beginning of the time known as the early Renaissance. During this period the famed Vatican Library began, and Leonardo da Vinci was born in 1452. Also at this time, a curious Portuguese prince was spending his days making maps and ocean charts, and sending out small boats to explore the west coast of Africa; this would pave the way for even greater adventures. He came to be called Henry the Navigator.

A strong Islamic military organization, the Ottoman Turks, had been steadily advancing and conquering the Byzantine territory, the last stronghold of the Eastern Empire. In 1453, they made their final conquest, the Christian city of Constantinople, renaming it Istanbul. The century-old empire now collapsed. It was at this point that the Christian Church was truly divided into two parts. The Roman Catholic Church was comprised mainly of Christians in western Europe, while Christians in Russia, Bulgaria, Greece, and Asia Minor made up the Orthodox Church. Five centuries later, we find the Churches still divided.

In the Roman Catholic Church, the common people had increased their devotion to the saints. Believing Jesus to be too inaccessible, they sought intercession through the saints, and especially Mary. Relics—bits of bone or clothing believed to have belonged to a saint—had been treasured for years, but now relic collecting became a hobby. The examples of the saints' lives and their relationship to God were often forgotten. Among Church leaders, attempts to deal with the conflict caused by the election of two popes led to a bigger crisis: the election of a third pope. In 1414, Holy Roman Emperor Sigismund decided his first task as leader was to settle this dispute. The four-year long Council of Constance resulted in the election of one pope, a Roman named Martin V.

During this time of discovery and progress in Europe, the advanced Chinese civilization began pulling back. The Ming dynasty stopped exploratory voyages and restricted foreign trade. These moves would result in a gradual falling behind at a time when Europeans were beginning to make strides both intellectually and geographically.

As the century progressed, sea voyages that would change the course of history began. In 1487, Bartholomeu Dias rounded the tip of Africa. In 1497, Vasco da Gama became the first European to reach India by sea. And of course, in 1492, Christopher Columbus set sail, with the backing of the strong leadership of Queen Isabella of Spain. In so doing, Columbus inadvertently stumbled onto a world which had existed for centuries, a world unknown to most people in Europe, Asia, and Africa.

These discoveries, however, did not drastically change the everyday lives of most Europeans. For Saint John of Kanty, daily existence meant living as Jesus had taught, calling many others to Jesus through his own example. He was ordained at age nineteen and became a professor of sacred Scripture. John was beloved and greatly respected not only by his students but by many in Krakow, where he befriended both the wealthy and the poor. He is a patron saint of Poland and Lithuania. His feast day is December 23.

The Story of John of Kanty

Here is a story of John of Kanty's unassuming yet loving ways. You might read this short story aloud yourself, or divide it among three readers.

Reader 1 Father John walked along the road on his way to dinner with friends. "Professor!" someone called.

Reader 2 John turned to see one of his students running up. "May I walk with you?" the young man asked. "I want to ask you to repeat what you said in class today, about fighting against things that are wrong."

Reader 3 "I said that we must fight false opinions, but your weapons must be patience, goodness, and love. Roughness spoils the best cause, and it is bad for your soul," John answered gently. Then noticing holes in the student's clothing, John pulled some coins out of his cloak. Pressing them into the hand of his companion, he said, "I must turn here. May God go with you."

Reader 1 "Thank you, Professor! All the students love and respect you greatly, and we poorer ones always know we can come to you for anything we need! Indeed, all the needy of Krakow know they can count on Father John!" John smiled humbly and answered, "I am only doing what Jesus asks."

Reader 2 They parted and soon John arrived at the large gate that secured the lavish home of his friends. John always chose to eat little, and never ate meat at all, but he was looking forward to the company of these friends. A servant appeared at the gate. John greeted him, but the man took one look at his patched, faded clothing and said, "I do not let any beggars in here! Go away!"

Reader 3 John shrugged, and smiled. He had given away the better clothing he owned to students in need. The servant glared at him, so John headed back to the university. He would begin preparing for next week's classes.

Reader 1   He had not gone far when two rough men stopped him. "Give us all your money!" one demanded. Without protest, John gave them what he had left. The robbers hastened off. Then John realized he had a few more coins.

Reader 2   "Wait!" he called, running after them. "I have more!" Astonished, the men stopped to watch as the priest approached them, a few coins in hand. "Take these, too," John said.

Reader 3   The thieves looked at one another, and one said, "No. Here, you can have all your money back. We are not going to keep it." They dropped the coins into John's open hand, and left hurriedly. John headed back to the university, praying for all those he had met that night.

Activities

1. This story would easily lend itself to a puppet show. Have some children create the puppets: Saint John, the student, the servant, and the two thieves. Draw them on tag board, or on paper that can be glued onto cardboard. The figures should be about twelve to sixteen inches tall. Using a strong tape, attach paint stir sticks, which can be obtained in a hardware store, to the backs of the puppets. Tape each stick high enough on the back of the puppet so it will not flop over, leaving enough stick free so that the puppeteer can easily manipulate the figure.

   One child or adult can read the story in its entirety, and others can work the puppets. A simple puppet theater can be made by standing a small folding table on its side, draping it with a blanket. Puppeteers sit behind it. Background scenery can be made by drawing scenes onto poster board, and placing the board in front of the table "theater." The narrator can change the scenes.

2. Bring in children's books about Christopher Columbus. Recently published books may present a more balanced picture of his actions and their repercussions in the Americas. Challenge children to debate the pros and cons of this subject, taking care to recognize that for some children this could be a sensitive topic.

Timeline

Using the information at the beginning of this chapter and in the story, add the fifteenth-century segment to your timeline.

More Saints of This Century

Bernardine of Siena (1380-1444); Frances of Rome (1384-1440); Joan of Arc (1412-1431); Francis of Padua (1413-1507); Casimir (1458-1483); Angela Merici (1474-1540); Jerome Emiliani (1481-1537).

Paul Miki

1564-1597

In the year 1500, a Portuguese explorer, Pedro Cabral, saw the coast of Brazil for the first time. Nineteen years later, another Portuguese man, Ferdinand Magellan, began the first trip around the world. This new knowledge of the world had many consequences, one of which was the discovery and invasion of the great Aztec and Inca nations by the Spanish.

The Spanish conquistadors arrived to find advanced and powerful cultures. The Aztec city of Tenochtitlan was home to half a million people, with stone temples, beautiful public buildings, palaces, and sprawling suburbs of houses. The Spanish, amazed by this splendor and sophistication, wanted to possess the riches they found there. Thus began years of attacks and resistance, but eventually the Spanish took control. The Aztec and Inca religions were banished, and sacred objects and temples were ruthlessly destroyed.

Christian missionaries arrived, trying to assist and win the dispirited people over to Christianity. One Aztec who did convert was a man named Cuatitlatoatzin, who took the name Juan Diego at his baptism. He was an impoverished widower living in a one-room, dirt-floor hut near present day Mexico City. One winter day in 1531, while walking fourteen miles to go to Mass, he heard beautiful music, then a voice calling him. A young woman appeared dressed as an Aztec princess. She spoke tenderly to Juan in his native language. Thus begins the story of the lady of Guadalupe, the appearance of Jesus' mother to the humble Juan. The signs she worked can still be seen today. Juan himself is said to have inspired the conversion of millions of Aztecs to Christianity in the years following his holy experience.

The sixteenth century saw the beginnings of a violent, inhuman practice: the kidnapping of Africans for the slave trade. From 1562 to 1568, a man named John Hawkins took cargoes of captives from west Africa to Hispaniola. The actions of Hawkins and others like him would greatly and adversely affect the lives of people of African descent for centuries to come.

In Europe, the age known as the Renaissance, or "rebirth," was bringing about much change. In the time between the fall of the Roman Empire and the fifteenth and sixteenth centuries, life for Europeans had been mainly a struggle for survival. Now, however, the political climate was stabilizing, trade was building up, and wealth accumulated for some. With more leisure time, the wealthier classes, and particularly those in Italy, began to look back to the Greek and Roman cultures. Learning once again became important, and discovering the beauty in people and nature was encouraged.

It was a time of new thinking, astonishing inventions in science, sea voyages into areas unknown by Europeans, and advances in painting, sculpture, architecture, and literature. Many of these artistic achievements were based on religious themes. Some of the illustrious artists that hail from this time are Leonardo da Vinci, Shakespeare, Michelangelo, Donatello, and Raphael.

Science saw great advances too, with da Vinci and Nicholas Copernicus, a Polish astronomer, among the best known. Copernicus declared that the earth revolved around the sun, and explained how long that took. This resulted in a change in the long-established calendar.

As world trade became more feasible, certain people amassed great wealth. It was through their support and interest that the arts and sciences flourished. Yet country folk lived hard, impoverished lives, often experiencing hunger and ill health due to poor nutrition. Those in towns fared better, where the larger community took pride in their town and cooperated to help one another. Working conditions were demanding, but the danger and drudgery of the Industrial Revolution was in the distant future, and guilds protected their workers.

The Renaissance brought the end of the Church's complete influence over the lives of Europeans. Those who studied the ancient Greek philosophers no longer looked at the world through the lens of the Church. They saw learning as a preparation for life, not salvation, as the Church taught. Many universities were started then which were not affiliated with the Church. Also, the affluent citizens did not want to hear that they should not store up riches, as the New Testament said.

In this time of renewal alongside unrest, the Roman Catholic Church was radically shaken by a movement that came to be known as the Reformation. The Catholic Church had entered a complex time in its history: there were many devotions that took precedence over a personal relationship with God. Fear of the Black Death and desire for salvation resulted in belief in the power of relics, and the business this belief fostered grew enormously. The popes and other officials led lavish and sometimes immoral lives; there was always a need for money as popes—who were essentially kings because they owned the papal states—needed to defend their land. Economics, politics, and bad theology had become entangled with Church teaching and exemplary living, and a German priest named Martin Luther felt the time had come for some changes.

On a chilly day in October of 1517, Luther walked to the church in his town of Wittenberg and nailed a poster to the church door that served as a community bulletin board. This poster outlined his challenges to the Church concerning the abuses it was perpetrating at the time. He did not intend to begin a movement that would splinter the Roman Catholic Church, but wanted to work within the Church for reform.

Luther hoped to bring the Church back to

its beginnings when Christians relied more on Scripture for guidance rather than on Church rules and regulations. But Luther's theory of justification by faith alone, combined with the politics of the time, entered in. When the papal officers saw Luther as a threat, German nobles protected him. By 1525, the movement that would become a separate religion named for Luther had grown and was out of his hands. It had become a power play between Church and state.

England had been Christian for more than twelve hundred years when Henry VIII became king. When he heard about Luther's attacks, Henry wrote a small book defending the teachings of the Catholic Church. For this, the pope gave him the title "Defender of the Faith."

When the pope denied Henry a divorce from his first wife, however, the king broke away from Rome and began the Church of England, based heavily on Catholicism but not under Roman authority. His six wives would suffer, Thomas More and John Fisher would die martyrs' deaths, and countless others, whether they were Roman Catholics or Reformers, would be persecuted. In the end, Henry's church triumphed. His son solidified the status of the Church of England during his six-year reign, and his daughter, Queen Elizabeth, who reigned from 1558 to 1603, would persecute Catholics.

Luther and other reformers intended to make changes within the Church, but they usually were not given a full hearing. Instead, the Catholic Church became defensive. Reformers like Luther and Henry VIII were dismayed and adamant, often striking back and separating themselves from the Church of Rome, leading to many dissensions and conflicts—as well as broad changes within Christianity. Some of these changes would bring pain and undue suffering to the Christian world, while others would eventually enhance it.

The Roman Catholic Church did seek its own reform at the Council of Trent. This brought about many healthy changes, some by reformers within the Church such as Teresa of Avila and Ignatius of Loyola. But these changes did not reunite the many factions. The Christian Church was now divided into many parts: Orthodox, Catholic, Lutherans, Calvinists, Anglicans (Church of England), and some smaller groups.

Despite all this upheaval and new directions within European Christianity, the Catholic Church was becoming a worldwide religion. Besides the mission work done in the Americas, Christianity was finding its way into Asia. The voyages of Spanish and Portuguese explorers led to trade with India, Sri Lanka, Indonesia, and Malaysia, and missionaries followed. Saint Francis Xavier preached in all these places.

In 1542, the first Portuguese merchants arrived in Japan. The missionaries who then arrived, including Xavier, made remarkable progress. By 1580, there were an estimated one hundred and fifty thousand Christians in Japan. The military leader, the shogun, saw this as a threat, and carried out a brief but violent persecution, almost wiping out Christianity in Japan entirely.

Among the first to die was a young man named Paul Miki. The martyrdom of Paul Miki and others took place at the end of the sixteenth century. After this persecution, the Japanese government enforced strict isolationist policies for two hundred years.

Here is the story of Paul and his faith, and that of his companions, those who died with him. Their feast day is February 6.

The Story of Paul Miki and Companions

The following story is told during the 1800s, when a French priest discovered a thriving underground Christian movement in Japan. Have the story read aloud with the help of a leader, two readers, and a chorus. The chorus lines are first read by the leader and repeated by the main group.

Leader Father Bernard Petitjean looked up from his work. A small group of Japanese people was approaching his house. He awaited them hopefully. For five years the French priest had worked here in Japan, trying to bring the news of Jesus to the Japanese people, with little result. Many years before, the rulers of Japan had sent home or killed many foreign Christian missionaries. The rulers had viewed the coming of a new religion as a threat to their power.

Reader 1 Only now, in the 1860s, were missionaries allowed into the country. But many of the Japanese people still felt fearful, thus making Father Petitjean's progress slow.

Reader 2 Father Petitjean greeted his visitors and invited them in. They seemed nervous, but then one woman began speaking softly, as if frightened.

Leader She spoke softly, as if frightened.

Chorus She spoke softly, as if frightened.

Reader 1 "Father," the woman said, "we are Christians. In secret, we say the prayers you say, celebrate the feast days, and baptize our children. We were taught all this by our parents, and they by their parents before them."

Reader 2 Startled, Father Petitjean said, "There has not been a Christian missionary here in two hundred years! Your families have kept the faith alive that long? Are there others besides you?"

"Oh, yes," the woman said, still speaking softly. "Many more. Hundreds, Perhaps thousands."

Leader Thousands of secret Christians!

Chorus Thousands of secret Christians!

Reader 1 "It began with the arrival of Francis Xavier in 1549," the woman said.

"Within a few decades, there were many Christians. The ruler, Hideyoshi, was jealous, fearful that they might take over. He watched them suspiciously.

Reader 2   "Among them was Father Paul Miki, who came from a wealthy Japanese family and had become a good preacher. When Hideyoshi decided to crush Christianity, Paul Miki was among the first to be arrested.

Reader 1   "On December 8, 1596, twenty-six men of Miako were condemned: three Japanese Jesuit priests, six Spanish Franciscan priests, and seventeen Japanese laymen. Among the laymen were teachers, doctors, and carpenters. And some were very young: there was a boy named Louis, who was ten years old; Anthony was thirteen; Thomas, sixteen; and Gabriel, nineteen.

Reader 2   "They were forced to walk more than three hundred miles from Miako to Nagasaki, through snow and ice. Along the way, they preached to many people who gathered to see them march. They sang psalms joyfully, and prayed the rosary, too.

Reader 1   "On February fifth, they reached Nagasaki, where twenty-six crosses awaited them. They were to die as their savior Jesus did. As Paul Miki hung on his cross, he forgave his persecutors, as Jesus had done before him."

Leader   He forgave his persecutors!

Chorus   He forgave his persecutors!

Reader 2   Here the woman paused. All were silent, but then she spoke again. "There were more persecutions after these deaths, about three thousand known martyrs. There were probably more who died, and still others who suffered imprisonment. The Church that had grown so rapidly at first was now just as rapidly destroyed. Or at least that is what the rulers thought.

Reader 1   "But secretly—underground you might say—the Church was kept alive. No missionaries were allowed into the country, but people quietly told their children, who told their children, who told their children…and here we are today."

Leader   They bravely kept the faith!

Chorus   They bravely kept the faith!

Activities

The sixteenth century was remarkable for the changes that came about worldwide. Here are some suggestions to help children better understand these times.

1. Explore the positive aspects of the Renaissance further. Find art books that show the magnificent work of artists such as Michelangelo, Raphael, Titian, da Vinci, and others. Two children's book biographies that are excellent are *The Bard of Avon: The Story of William Shakespeare,* by Diane Stanley and Peter Vennema, and *Leonardo da Vinci,* by Diane Stanley.

2. The sixteenth century was an extremely difficult one for the Roman Catholic Church. Perhaps because of this, the list of saints from this time is impressive. In times of stress, it is always helpful to be able to laugh—a fact that was as true in the sixteenth century as it is today.

    Introduce children to two saints who did their great works with a sense of humor. Saint Philip Neri had two favorite books: one was the New Testament, the other a book of jokes and riddles. Challenge children to find out why Philip shaved off half of his beard, and what he did with the cardinal's hat the pope gave him. Saint Teresa of Avila, who had the very real honor of being the first woman named as a Doctor of the Church, also had a humorous side, and is even said to have joked with Jesus. Help children find this story.

Timeline

Using the information in the introduction and the story from this chapter, add the sixteenth-century segment to your timeline.

More Saints of This Century

John Fisher (1469-1535); Juan Diego (1474-1548); Thomas More (1478-1535); Cajetan (1440-1557); Ignatius of Loyola (c. 1491-1556); John of God (1495-1550); Anthony Zaccaria (1502-1539); Francis Xavier (1506-1552); Philip Neri (1515-1595); Teresa of Avila (1515-1582); Peter Canisius (1521-1597); Turibius of Mogrovejo (1538-1691); Charles Borromeo (1538-1584); John of the Cross (1542-1591); Lawrence of Brindisi (1559-1619); Aloysius Gonzaga (1568-1591).

Martin de Porres
1579-1639

Peter Claver
1581-1654

Kateri Tekakwitha
1656-1680

In the seventeenth century, John Milton wrote *Paradise Lost.* Ice cream became popular in Paris. Bach and Handel were born, and cheddar cheese was first made. Isaac Newton invented the reflecting telescope, and Louis XIV began building the Palace of Versailles.

The Thirty Years War began in Germany with conflicts between Protestants and Catholics; but it soon became a struggle to determine if the powerful Hapsburg family of Austria would gain control of Germany. Catholic Emperor Ferdinand II of Austria thought he could beat the Protestant Prussians. King Gustavus of Sweden, however, sided with the Protestants. Even leaders in Catholic France allied with the Protestants, for they were afraid that if Austria won, Germany would unite against France.

The war finally ended in 1648, and the religious lines of Europe were drawn: Scandinavia, Prussia, and parts of southern Germany were Lutheran; Switzerland, much of Holland, and Scotland were Calvinist; England had its own

Church; and the rest of Europe was predominantly Catholic. The Thirty Years War brought both the Holy Roman Empire and the Hapsburg dynasty into a position of equality with, not superiority over, the monarchies of France, Sweden, England, Spain, and the Dutch Republic. The way for the present state system in Europe was made clear.

The Renaissance continued, with lavish churches built in a style called baroque. But some Roman Catholics were establishing a religious life based on service to the needs of those who were poor, sick, or homeless. Saint Vincent de Paul founded hospitals, schools, and orphanages, and brought about prison reform. He organized groups of laypeople for charitable work, educating many wealthy people to reach out to those in need. He and Saint Louise de Marillac founded the Daughters (or Sisters) of Charity.

Saint John Baptist de la Salle began the first teaching order, and changed the face of education forever. He had the revolutionary idea that giving poor children a practical education would improve their lives. At this time, only wealthy children were educated, in Latin, in very small groups by tutors. De la Salle began teaching in classrooms filled with students, in the children's own language.

Science in seventeenth-century Europe was a mixture of discovery, fear, violence, courage, superstition, and hope. Copernicus's theory was still not accepted by the Church, whose interpretation of the Bible held that the earth was the center of the solar system, not the sun as Copernicus had stated. Galileo, the brilliant Italian mathematician, astronomer, and physicist made remarkable progress in his fields. But he was met with great opposition from the Church because his theories supported Copernicus. The Inquisition, a tribunal of the Catholic Church which secretly tried and often violently punished those suspected of heresy, was in use. Galileo faced this tribunal more than once, and he spent his last years under house arrest.

Potatoes and tobacco from the Americas were introduced in England. A bald man might apply a mixture of garlic, honey, and wormwood to his head in hopes of growing hair. And, forty-five years after Galileo's death, Newton discovered the law of gravity.

In Japan, this century brought stability after a lack of leadership. The shogun and military leader was in power. A boy slated to become an esteemed samurai warrior was trained in archery and wrestling, but also in calligraphy, dance, painting, and floral arrangement. He was expected to be a peaceful Buddhist when not a fierce warrior on the battlefield.

A child in India, whose father was an elephant keeper for the Emperor Akbur, would help wash the elephants in the river. A great procession was planned for the emperor, in which the elephants were to take part. The child would help secure a fringed and embroidered bonnet on each elephant's head, then place a woven cloth over the elephant's back. A follower of Hinduism, this child would be a vegetarian and would enjoy *chapati*, or bread, with his rice, peas, limes, and lentils.

In Russia, Peter the Great was working to modernize as well as expand his country. The Persians and Turks suffered sixteen years of war with one another. A French Jesuit, Alexander de Rhodes, worked in Asia, bringing Christianity to Viet Nam.

The seventeenth century saw further expansion by Europeans. Colonization was underway in Central and South America by Spain and Portugal; and now the French, English, and Dutch were exploring the northern hemisphere. Most of this was done by private companies, and there was much rivalry among them. In 1620, the Mayflower landed at Plymouth. On board were Puritans, a Christian pilgrim group escaping the religious intolerance of England.

The Native Americans had already experienced great hardship at the hands of Europeans. The Patuxet man, Squanto, famous for his kindness and assistance to the hungry Pilgrims, had been kidnapped twice by the English and taken to Europe as a slave. When he returned, he found his people had all died of the European illness, smallpox. The year before the Pilgrims arrived, the first African slaves had been brought to Virginia.

And so, the culture and people of the Americas were becoming diversified. So, too, were the Christians who lived and worked there. Three exceptional ones were Martin de Porres, whose feast day is November 3; Peter Claver, September 9; and Kateri Tekakwitha, July 14.

The Story of Martin de Porres, Peter Claver, and Kateri Tekakwitha

For this story you will need an adult narrator, three children for storytellers, and a prayer leader. Set up three unlit candles before the storytelling begins. An adult should supervise the candle lighting.

Narrator   In the seventeenth century, there were many Christians in the Americas. Here are stories of three saints from this time who lived their Christianity in different places and ways.

MARTIN DE PORRES

Martin de Porres lived in Peru. He was a very intelligent and cheerful child despite a hard life. Martin's mother was a free Black woman and his father a Spanish nobleman who abandoned her and his son. Martin was often treated unfairly because of his dual heritage, and he was very poor. At age twelve, Martin became a barber. Barbers then did medical work as well as cut hair. Martin had a great talent for healing. Sick people and even animals came to him for help.

When he was fifteen, Martin entered a monastery as a lowly lay helper. Perhaps because of his painful childhood Martin did not believe he was capable of much, but others saw how talented and spiritual Martin was. Martin loved Jesus and Mary very much, and he valued life in all its forms. He brought sick people off the streets to care for them, he took in injured animals, and he planted fruit trees along the roads for hungry people. He started orphanages and hospitals, and he cared for Africans forced to come to Peru as slaves.

Here is a story about Martin:

Martin had just finished dishing up soup for more than one hundred people. Each day, there seemed to be more and more hungry people who found their way to Martin's kettle at the monastery door. Now he hurried to his job in the monastery hospital. There Martin saw the brother who was his boss holding up a sheet. "Look! Mice have chewed holes in the bedding! We'll put out poison right now!" he said. Martin touched the sheet. "The poor mice!" he said. "They aren't given their daily meals like us, so they eat our sheets."

Just then, a tiny gray mouse scurried past and Martin scooped up the trembling animal. Stroking it, Martin said: "I know you are hungry, little one, but your chewing is harming the sick folks here. Gather all your friends, move into the garden, and I'll bring you food every day so long as you leave the sheets alone."

Martin bent down and released the mouse. Instantly, there was a rustling sound, and from under the wardrobe, from the joists in the ceiling, from every crack in the floor, mice emerged. Finally, when no more came out of hiding, the whole group of mice ran out to the garden hedges. The brother laughed and shook his head in wonder. Martin smiled. And he kept his promise. Each day, after he had served dinner to the sick, to the other brothers, and to the poor at the door, Martin brought dinner to the mice. From then on there were no new holes in the sheets, but quite a few in among the garden hedges.

Narrator   Saint Martin de Porres, please help us to see our own talents, and to learn to use them to help others. *Light one candle.*

All   Saint Martin de Porres, pray for us.

PETER CLAVER

Peter Claver was born in Spain, but when he was twenty-nine, this Jesuit priest traveled across the ocean to a place we call Colombia. There he was horrified by the slave trade: the practice of kidnapping African people, forcing them into ships where they were badly mistreated, bringing them to Colombia and other places, and selling them as slaves. Peter spent the next forty years working for the Africans and against slavery. This was very difficult work, but Peter had great energy, and he prayed constantly. His love for Jesus made it possible for him to work among these suffering African people.

Here is a story about Peter:

Claver walked through the streets of Cartagena. All around him were misery, greed, and evil, for this was the scene of a large slave trade. A ship had just come in, bringing more Africans who were chained below the decks, starving, sick, and frightened. Soon they would be herded like cattle into warehouses and sold as slaves. Peter was going to that ship, to bring food, medicine, and his care.

In the streets, he saw many people connected with this vile business: hotels were filled with buyers, offices bustled with salespeople and bookkeepers. Shuddering, Peter began to pray. Suddenly, a man stepped out in front of him, blocking his way. Peter recognized him as a large landholder who had many slaves. Leaning into Peter's face, the man said roughly, "Stay out of the slave business, Father. Your business is with the Church."

"These people you enslave are God's children. The Church teaches that, and Pope Paul III has spoken out against slavery. The Church calls upon me to cry out against this sin," Peter said.

He wondered how many times he had already said this to others. The man backed away but stood glaring at Peter. Peter shifted his heavy sack laden with food and medical supplies and walked on. At the dock, he would have to persuade the ship's captain to let him in, but with Jesus' help, he would. As he moved along, Peter prayed for the strength to face the misery he would see there. He prayed that he would be calm and caring, bandaging wounds and giving food and drink without weeping himself.

The wind picked up a little. Soon it would be colder and the ships would stop sailing for this year. Peter would move to the mines or plantations where Africans were enslaved. There he would confront those in power, like the man who had stopped him today. With Jesus' help, Peter would continue to chip away at this evil called slavery for a long time.

Narrator   Saint Peter Claver, please help us to have the courage to fight against what is wrong. *Light the second candle.*

All   Saint Peter Claver, pray for us.

KATERI TEKAKWITHA

Far to the north of where Peter and Martin lived, a girl named Tekakwitha was born to the Mohawk people. Her father was the chief. Her mother, who was Algonquin, had become Christian. Many of the native peoples were fearful of Christians, for hurtful things had been done to them by persons who called themselves Christians. Tekakwitha's mother understood this, so she told her small daughter the stories of Jesus only when they were alone.

When Tekakwitha was four years old, smallpox swept through her village. As the little girl lay ill, her parents and brother died. Tekakwitha survived, but her eyesight was damaged, her body weakened, and her face scarred. Her mother's friend who cared for her told her more stories about the Christian God. Then Tekakwitha went to live in her uncle's village, where she was raised by her aunts. Despite her weakness, she was kind, gentle, and helpful, and others greatly loved her.

But Tekakwitha felt God's love even more. She chose to be baptized, taking the Christian name of Catherine, or Kateri. Her decision to become Christian puzzled and angered some of her people. She secretly left her village, traveling for days to reach a Christian settlement. There she went to Mass daily, prayed frequently, cared for the sick, and taught the children. All who knew her were astonished by her love of God. Always weak in health, Kateri Tekakwitha died at the age of twenty-four. Her last words were, "Jesus, I love you."

Here is a story about Kateri:

Tekakwitha quietly walked along the shores of the water. She had no idea that in far-off places, there were people who chose to live away from others and spend their time in prayer. She did not have a Bible or prayerbooks. She had few people to talk to about God and Jesus. But somehow, she knew God's love and felt it strongly. Whether she was near the gently rippling water, walking under the fragrant pine trees of the forest, or even working in the midst of the busy village life, Tekakwitha felt God with her.

The others of her village found her odd. They became frustrated with her because she refused to marry, saying God was the only one she could love. Her body was weak and her eyes often hurt. But none of this mattered, for Tekakwitha lived and worked only for the love of God.

Narrator   Blessed Kateri Tekakwitha, please teach us that God is always with us. *Light the third candle.*

All   Blessed Kateri Tekakwitha, pray for us.

Activities

1. Martin lived in Lima, Peru; Peter worked in Colombia; Kateri Tekakwitha lived near Auriesville, New York, and Montreal, Canada. Help children understand the diversity of Christianity in the Americas by having them locate these places on the map. Small drawings or symbols of the saints could be placed on the map. As children learn of other holy people in the Americas, add these to the map.

2. The Native American people of the 1600s, particularly those of the upper Midwest, passed on their culture and history through storytelling. Grandparents told children legends and funny tales during the long winter months. History was recorded by symbolic drawings on deerskin of significant events.

   Encourage the children to ask questions about their extended families and to make a family history book by drawing. Perhaps an elder in their family would draw with them. If family histories are not feasible, fascinating facts about the early years of their towns or their parishes could be researched.

Timeline

Using the information at the beginning of this chapter and in the story, add the seventeenth-century segment to your timeline.

More Saints of This Century

Francis de Sales (1567-1622); Josaphat (c. 1580-1623); Vincent de Paul (1580-1660); John de Brebeuf (1593-1649); Lawrence Ruiz (1600-1637); Joseph of Cupertino (1602-1663); John Baptiste de la Salle (1651-1719).

Elizabeth Ann Seton

1774-1821

The eighteenth century brought many new inventions: merry-go-rounds, pocket watches, machine guns, steam engines, fountain pens, threshing machines, telegraphs, pianofortes, and porcelain. Oxygen was discovered. A London residence for the British prime minister was built at 10 Downing Street. The Rococo art movement was in vogue. The Louvre became a national art gallery.

When the century first dawned, the Pitjantuatjara people were living in the desert of what would later be called Australia. A nomadic people, they followed their ancestors' ways, setting up camps at each stop. They lived by hunting kangaroo, lizards, and snakes, and gathering berries, roots, and seeds, which were ground between two stones to produce flour.

Christianity was introduced in Korea, while Chinese Christians were facing a crisis. The Jesuits had been working in China, and by 1660, Mass was being said in Chinese, not Latin. Other missionaries raised objections, and in 1704, Pope Clement XI banned the Chinese Mass. He said that Chinese Christians should adopt Western customs along with the religion, as had been expected of the native people in other missionary lands. Emperor K'ang-hsi was insulted and immediately outlawed all missionary work, ordering all the Jesuits out of China. Chinese Catholics felt abandoned. Many were persecuted, some were executed. Church power was diminishing elsewhere, too, because of the efforts of monarchs who wanted more control, particularly in France.

There was an even more potent movement that affected the Catholic Church, as well as the future of millions of people. It was called the Enlightenment. This intellectual movement, led by philosophers such as Voltaire and Rousseau and fed by scientists like Newton, nourished a yearning for knowledge and a scientific mentality, along with a strong desire to throw off all traditions that restrained this learning.

The Enlightenment, also called the Age of Reason, encouraged acquiring knowledge and beliefs through reasoning, not by blind adherence to prescribed doctrines or rules. Some proponents taught that the universe was ordered completely and reasonably, and this order could be explained by science alone, not by religion.

Others, like Benjamin Franklin, held to a belief in God. Still others stated that human beings, not God, were at the center of the universe. They all wanted religious tolerance, freedom of speech, education for all classes as a way to combat ignorance and prejudice, and an end to slavery. The Enlightenment was an ideology that became almost a religion to some of its followers. It was a call for freedom, democracy, and equality.

Despite these noble goals, the Enlightenment, like the Renaissance, was an elitist movement, often allied with people who had money and power. Still, its effects were far reaching. Because of it, Christianity's role in European life was lessened. Religion became detached from civil life, and an individual's beliefs were no longer the business of the state, a change from Renaissance thinking.

The idea of a secular society was radical. Religion, science, and education began to go their separate ways. The Catholic Church, for the most part, refused to come to terms with these trends, which challenged Christian tradition and biblical interpretation. Two revolutions were justified on the basis of Enlightenment beliefs in natural human rights, first in North America and then in France.

Native peoples and a variety of Europeans had been vying for land and power for a long time in the Americas. By the 1770s, the British held great control over their colonies in eastern North America, and the colonists resented this. A strong resistance to the commercial power Britain held over them, as well as anti-monarchy sentiment, fueled the resentment and led to the war that resulted in the establishment of the United States of America. The new country would be founded on the ideals of democracy.

American independence was recognized in 1783, as conditions for a revolution were ripening in France. This revolution would last from 1789 to 1799, and would put an end to the French monarchy.

The Enlightenment ideals of democracy and equality became a rallying cry of the oppressed, but what followed was a level of violence that had not been foreseen. The French Catholic Church was one of the targets for numerous reasons, including the lavish lifestyles of many of the clergy, and the Church's stance against capitalism, an economic system which would benefit the middle class. And so, in September of 1792, French revolutionaries killed between eleven hundred and fifteen hundred priests.

Over the course of the revolution, about seventeen thousand people died. One by one, different groups came into power in France, then lost that power to another group. Also in 1792, France offered to aid people of other countries who wanted to overthrow their governments. Soon, France was at war with most of Europe. As the century ended, this French movement showed no signs of stopping as a new leader emerged. His name was Napoleon Bonaparte.

In New York City, one year before the American Revolution, Elizabeth Ann Bayley (later Seton), was born. Her family was wealthy, and were Episcopalians dedicated to studying Scripture and helping those less fortunate. Elizabeth, however, was destined to live a life of simplicity within the Catholic Church. She was the first person born in the United States to be declared a saint. Her feast day is January 4.

The Story of Elizabeth Ann Seton

The story is told from the viewpoint of seven people who knew Elizabeth Seton at different points in her life. Choose seven readers for the parts.

Reader 1   I am Elizabeth's aunt. After her mother died, Betty, as we call her, came to live with us here at the seashore. She was born in New York City, when the war, the Revolution, was about to begin. Life is unsettled for our young country, but I try to provide the children with a good education. Betty is a lively, pretty child and very intelligent. Her father, a professor and a doctor, has taught her to aid those who have less than we do. He often works with the sick and poor immigrants who come to New York. Her grandfather was a rector for Saint Andrew's Episcopal Church on Staten Island, and we have all taught Betty our religion well.

I am pleased that she spends time alone frequently, reading the Bible. But I am also proud that she can speak French, play the piano, and ride a horse. I am teaching her how to manage a large household and servants. She must learn all the skills that a young lady of her social status will need. In a few years, our dear Betty will be old enough for the dances given for young people of marriageable age. I want to be sure she is ready for the grand life she has ahead of her.

Reader 2   I am a friend of Elizabeth Bayley. She has returned from her uncle's home to live with her father here in New York City, our nation's capital. It is an exciting time, for the famous General Washington will soon be inaugurated as our first president! But Elizabeth and I are also excited about the many parties that will be held for the young ladies of well-to-do families. Perhaps we will meet our future husbands at these balls!

Elizabeth is so intelligent, quick, and pretty that everyone likes her. She and I dress in our beautiful gowns, and giggle over which young men will ask us to dance. Elizabeth does not have to wonder too much, for they flock to her. But there is one in particular she likes—William

Seton. And, I can tell by the way he hurries over to her, that he feels the same way!

Reader 3   I am Mrs. Seton's servant. I have been with the Setons ever since they were married. Mrs. Seton was only nineteen then, but she was more than able to run this large, beautiful house. She and Mr. Seton are a very happy, loving couple. His shipping business is successful, so money is plentiful. So are the children! First there is Anna Maria, then Rebecca, Bill, Dick, and now baby Kit. Besides her motherly and household duties, Mrs. Seton raises money and even sews clothes for the poor immigrant people here in New York City. She says she learned to do this work from her father, Doctor Bayley.

Reader 4   I am Elizabeth's friend, and I am very concerned about her. Everything seems to be going wrong for that good woman! First, William's brother died. William and Elizabeth decided to take in his five children and Elizabeth herself teaches all ten children in their home. Then her father died. Next, William's business failed. I am certain they have many bills.

And now, William is sick. He seems to have that terrible disease, tuberculosis. His doctor has recommended a sea voyage for his health, and Elizabeth has just told me she is selling their home and all their possessions so she can afford to take him to Italy! I know the warm climate will be good for him, and they have friends there, but I see the sadness in Elizabeth's eyes. I know she will cope with the loss of money, though I cannot imagine how. But if she should lose her beloved William…I worry for them.

Reader 5   I am Elizabeth's Italian friend. We have just said our good-byes and she is on the ship back to New York. I am praying for her. She came here with hopes of a cure for William, but he died shortly after they arrived. We helped her in every way we could. She stayed with us after his death, and seemed to find great comfort in our religion, which is Roman Catholic. She spent much time going into our beautiful churches to pray. Often she asked me questions, particularly about the Eucharist and our devotion to Jesus' mother. I know she turned to God to overcome her sorrow.

I hope her faith will continue to be a comfort to her, for she returns now to her children, without their father, and without much money. It is a good thing she has family to rely on.

Reader 6 I am Elizabeth's cousin. What can she be thinking of? She returns home, grieving for her husband, and announces she has decided to become a Catholic! The family is appalled. We told her to forget this idea, or we would have nothing to do with her. Of course, I thought that would bring her to her senses—she cannot raise those children, penniless as she is, without her family's help! But she will not give up this plan. Most of her friends are deserting her, too, though one has provided her with the upstairs rooms of a small house. There she lives with her five children. What will become of them?

Reader 7 I am a sister in the order called the Daughters of Charity of Saint Vincent de Paul. We are the first order of sisters begun in America, founded by Elizabeth Seton, or Mother Seton, as we call her. It all began when a priest in Baltimore heard about her, and asked her to come to his city, where there are many Catholics, to start a school. Poor girls and African Americans—people not usually educated—came to Mother Seton for schooling. It was the first Catholic school in America. Then she began our order. We lived simply, sharing what we had with the children who came to us. We also visited the sick, and helped poor families of the area.

More and more women joined us, and soon bishops were asking Mother Seton to send her sisters to other cities, to work there. She began more schools, hiring teachers, even writing textbooks. She started the first Catholic hospital in America, as well as the first Catholic orphanage. She has accomplished a tremendous amount in a few years, while caring for her own children. Yet, she has lost so much—her daughters Anna Maria and Rebecca both died of tuberculosis, as their father did. And now, we fear, she too suffers from it. But for now, her faith keeps her going, as she tells us, "In doing our daily work, strive first to do the will of God, to do it as God wills it to be done, and to do it because it is God's will."

Activities

1. Elizabeth had to weather tremendous changes in her lifetime. Instead of being devastated by her many losses, she rose to the challenges in creative and courageous ways. Discuss with children the fact that all people have challenges in their lives. Ask them to think of their own and write down how they can meet them. Together, compose a prayer asking for guidance and strength to meet life's difficulties.

2. To celebrate the musical accomplishments of the eighteenth century, listen to recordings of music of Bach, Beethoven, Mozart, and others.

Timeline

Using the information at the beginning of this chapter and in the story, add the eighteenth-century segment to your timeline.

More Saints of This Century

Paul of the Cross (1694-1775); Alphonsus Liguori (1696-1787); Maria Marguerite d'Youville (1701-1771); Junípero Serra (1713-1784); Julia Billiart (1751-1816).

John Bosco

1815-1888

Lake Harriet lay placid and sparkling under the summer sun. Several children, hair and clothing dripping after a swim, sat near a small fire where their turtle soup simmered. Soon they would be called to help with the corn harvest, but for today, they laughed and teased each other in the Dakota language as they cooked their meal.

Among the dark-haired Dakota children sat a Dutch-American child named Jane DeBow, who chatted with them effortlessly. She had come from New York with Protestant missionaries who hoped to convert the Dakota people living in what would become Minnesota. Here Jane had found a new family, for she was greatly loved by the Dakotas.

As an adult, Jane would watch with sadness as her Dakota friends' lives were challenged by changes caused by white settlement. It would not be the only major change for this vast country over the course of the century. Some of the happenings were: a war between the United States and Mexico; twenty-eight new

states entering the Union; industrialization in the eastern states; immigrants arriving by the thousands; European-American settlement of lands well beyond Minnesota; unrest about issues such as slavery that led to a split in the country then to the Civil War in the 1860's; and the upheaval and reorganization that followed.

Life was complicated and demanding in other parts of the world, too. In 1804, Napoleon Bonaparte was crowned emperor. His overwhelming ambition led to a series of wars from 1803 to 1815, involving Britain, Russia, Austria, Sweden, Portugal, and Prussia. Toward the middle of the century, there was much unrest in Europe, with food shortages and nationalist feelings leading to revolts.

Still, in the latter half of the century, European countries were able to seize power in other parts of the world. Britain, with Queen Victoria on the throne, annexed thirty-nine separate territories, including India. Africa, the part of the world most vulnerable to European power, was partitioned up among Britain, France, Germany, Portugal, Belgium, Spain, and Italy.

In Korea, Catholicism was taking hold, despite persecutions. About ten thousand Catholics were martyred there before religious liberty was declared; among these martyrs were Saints Andrew Kim and Paul Chong Hasang. In the 1850s, the number of Catholics in Korea was estimated at two hundred thousand, despite persecution. The number of Catholics also grew in the Philippines, Hong Kong, Sri Lanka, Malaysia, Burma, Thailand, and India. In Africa, Catholicism increased in Tanzania, Uganda, Zaire, Zambia, and Kenya.

Under Pope Pius IX, the long debated subject of Mary's immaculate conception became dogma. And at the First Vatican Council (1869-1870), doctrine regarding the pope's infallibility was also accepted as dogma, as well. Charles Darwin's book, *Origin of Species*, caused much controversy within the Church, and Pope Leo XIII instituted a Vatican biblical commission to apply these new methods and ideas to Bible study.

Yet in the midst of this upheaval, beauty and culture prevailed. Hans Christian Andersen was spinning tales that would touch the hearts of millions of children; Beatrix Potter, a young English girl, began drawing and painting delightful pictures of flowers and animals. Claude Monet, Pierre-Auguste Renoir, Paul Cezanne, Mary Cassatt, and others were creating works of art called Impressionism.

The driving force of many of the changes at this time was the Industrial Revolution. It actually had its beginnings in eighteenth-century Britain, with the invention of the flying shuttle. This machine enabled weavers to produce cloth more quickly and in greater width than ever before. Because of their large size, the machines were housed in big buildings called factories. Other technologies developed. Improvements on the steam engine resulted in greater power, speeding up production. People engaged in cottage industries were unable to produce enough goods to compete, and were forced to work in factories. Soon towns sprang up around the factories.

As with all major changes, the Industrial Revolution brought both good and bad. Advances were made in science, particularly in areas involving gas, oil, electricity, and chemical engineering. Transportation improved. Louis Pasteur discovered germs and promoted the theory that cleanliness and health were connected. Vast and positive changes in public health eventually resulted from his discoveries.

However, the Industrial Revolution was the major cause of many of these health problems. Factory workers, including children, worked in unsafe, unhealthy conditions for fifteen hours a day. Polluted drinking water was used, causing epidemics of dysentery, typhoid, and cholera. Rheumatism, bronchitis, anemia, rickets, and tuberculosis were common. People of various professions and beliefs voiced their concern, among them: Charles Dickens, Cardinal Manning, Karl Marx, Friedrich Engels, Pope Leo XIII, Jane Addams, and many others.

With a style all his own, a young Italian priest named John Bosco championed the rights of children caught in the miseries of the Industrial Revolution. He is remembered for his innovative work with boys, and for the religious order he founded (the Salesians) to promote his mission. His exuberance spilled over into his work, as did his talents, his faith, and his love of life. John Bosco's feast day is January 31.

The Story of John Bosco

Saint John Bosco's story is told here by his mother, who worked with him. Have an adult with a flair for storytelling narrate it, encouraging children to respond to the questions.

My name is Margaret Bosco. Have you heard of my son, Father John Bosco? He was not yet two when his father died. I was left to care for my three boys and my aged mother, and to run our farm. We were very poor, but even as I struggled to feed my family, I marveled at John. He never held still if there was something to learn. What a wiggler! Were any of you wigglers when you were toddlers?

Pause for children's responses.

When John got to be your age, he loved going to fairs. He studied the magician's tricks very closely, and then he would imitate them! He watched those daredevil acrobats perform their stunts. Back at home, he would practice what he saw. Oh, I had to close my eyes! I couldn't bear to watch him fall. The bumps and bruises he had would make you shudder. He even learned tightrope walking. What a child! But you know, he got to be very good at those tricks, even better than the acrobats he watched. Can any of you do a cartwheel?

Pause for children's responses.

When he was nine, John knew he wanted to become a priest when he grew up. I could not afford to send him to school for that, but I encouraged him in his dream. I knew God had plans for him. He was growing up now, taller than I, with a rich crop of curly, chestnut hair. He was cheerful, loving, and a hard worker. Of course, he had his faults, too. He was so full of energy and enthusiasm that he sometimes did things too quickly, without thinking. He had strong emotions, and once in a while, he settled an argument with his fists. He felt badly after those incidents. Have you ever done something you regretted?

Pause for children's responses.

Soon he was old enough to go the seminary, wearing a hand-me-down suit. John worked many jobs in order to afford school, but his quick learning served him well. I'll name some jobs he did and you tell me which you think he liked the best: making candy, repairing shoes, managing a restaurant, and putting on a one-man circus.

Pause for children's responses.

Yes, the one-man circus was his favorite. Children gathered to watch, and he'd slip in a religion lesson or two. When John completed his seminary classes, he was required to work in hospitals, prisons, and orphanages. John knew what it meant to be poor, but the suffering he saw broke his tender heart. Mostly, he worried about the boys he had seen. You see, many had left poor homes and were now living on the city streets, some working long, hard jobs, like carrying bricks up five stories, fifty times a day. Some had no work, so they were always hungry, scared, and cold.

John attracted a small group of boys by doing tricks like tightrope walking and juggling. They were delighted. Then he gave them food, and soon he had them praying. These boys brought their friends, who brought their friends. The number kept growing and growing. John used all his energy and creativity to help the boys. Then he got sick and almost died from pneumonia. The boys were terrified. Some hung about the hospital, others went to pray. They organized 'round-the-clock prayer vigils, and many fasted. John recovered quite miraculously. When he left the hospital, the boys raced to him, picked him up, and carried him through the streets, singing, shouting, and cheering. Have you ever been worried about someone you love?

Pause for children's responses.

John had plans to start a home for these boys. Many people were against his work, for they did not want these loud, possibly violent boys around. John thought that if I came to help, his household would be better accepted. So I began to work there; I cleaned, washed and mended clothing, cooked, planted vegetables, and took care of sick children. The boys called me Mama Margaret.

Of course John worked, too. He taught the boys religion, reading, math, geography, grammar, drawing, and singing. He trained teachers to help as the number of boys kept growing. He wrote books during the night to help support us. He cut the boys' hair. He ran races with them, joked with them, challenged them in conversation. And he prayed with them. Through his love and care, he helped them see that our God is a loving God. Is there someone who helps you learn about God?

Pause for children's responses.

When John was a child, so full of energy, I knew God had plans for all his talent, and I encouraged John to learn what God's plan was. I encourage you now to learn and to pray, and to ask what God's plan is for you, too.

Activities

1. Put on a John Bosco fair. Model it after a backyard fair: organize a fishing booth, ring toss game, face painting, etc., and have a storytime or puppet show telling Bible stories. If you choose to collect money for this, you might donate it to an organization that works for children living in poverty.

2. John Bosco felt strongly that the children he worked with needed a trade to rise from poverty and feel confidence in themselves. He also believed that God had plans for each of them. Talk with children about careers and vocations. List possibilities and talk about how people can use their talents to better the world.

3. The 1800s were a diverse time in the history of the United States; this time period is a frequent topic in children's literature. One series of historical fiction that helps young readers understand children's experiences at that time is the *Dear America* series by Scholastic. Some of the titles are *A Line in the Sand* (1836), *Across the Wide and Lonesome Prairie* (1847), *A Picture of Freedom* (1859), *I Thought My Soul Would Rise and Fly* (1865), and *West to a Land of Plenty* (1883).

Timeline

Using the information at the beginning of this chapter and in the story, add the nineteenth-century segment to your timeline.

More Saints of This Century

Rose Philippine Duchesne (1769-1852); John Vianney (1786-1859); Andrew Kim, Paul Chong Hasang and Companions (d. 1821-1846); Peter Chanel (1803-1841); John Neumann (1811-1860); Bernadette Soubirous (1844-1879); Frances Cabrini (1850-1917); Thérèse of Lisieux (1873-1891); Charles Lwanga (d. 1886).

Edith Stein

1891-1942

Perhaps historians will look back on the twentieth century and say that the underlying theme of that time was change—not the gentle, plodding change from season to season, but rapid, dizzying, turbulent change.

A European emigrating to the United States in the early part of the century would likely have left behind a life of poverty, perhaps a thatched-roof home lighted with kerosene lamps, with no running water, and with simple, minimal food. Education may have been minimal too, and epidemics and war would have touched her life. She would arrive at Ellis Island after a grueling passage by ship, with only one suitcase and little money. Later, after she had settled into work in a city factory or on a farm in a rural area, she felt confidence in her new country. She prayed in church, her head covered with a veil, at a Latin Mass. This new American looked forward to a happy, modest future.

By the latter years of this century, that immigrant might have grandchildren who traveled by air, owned two cars at once, earned college degrees, ran parish councils, read Scripture at the pulpit at an English-language Mass, benefitted from advanced medical care, and worried about their children's safety in schools. They were also alarmed about the possibilities of nuclear war, warmed their abundant convenience foods in a microwave oven, questioned the politics of their government, gave their preschoolers free access to their personal computers, and watched movies at the push of a button.

What happened in the course of a century to cause such differences?

War was one of the factors. Pick any decade of this century and you will find a war or revolution. Sadly, there is nothing new about the frequency of war or the human ability to kill and destroy. But in the twentieth century, advances in technology led to new, unimagined horrors. The Great War, or World War I, brought a new understanding of how far-reaching war can be. In Europe it was fought on three fronts, and it was also fought in the Middle East, and at sea. The Russian Revolution occurred during this time, too. New weapons and methods heightened the violence. Poison gas, the tank, the airplane, and trench warfare all led to appalling numbers of casualties: about forty million lives were lost.

That war was supposed to end all wars, but it actually led to another, even more devastating war. Between the first and second world wars, many parts of the world were left in deep economic difficulty. Unemployment and hunger haunted many. The German people were especially depleted because of the way their country had been dealt with after World War I. In Spain, there was a bloody civil war.

Adolf Hitler, Benito Mussolini, and Francisco Franco came into power in Europe. Soon, people who had not yet recovered from the ravages of one war were caught in another. World War II began in 1939 when Germany invaded Poland. It lasted until 1945. On one side were the Axis Powers, Germany, Italy, and Japan. Britain, France, the Soviet Union, China, and the United States were on the other side, known as the Allied Powers. This war was fought in four main areas: Europe, Asia, Africa, and at sea. An estimated fifty-five million people died.

The weapons for World War II were even more advanced than those used in World War I. The atomic bomb was dropped on Japan. The United States' use of this bomb ended this terrible war, but the dire implications for the Japanese people, and indeed for the entire world, were not fully imagined before that fateful day in August of 1945. There was another aspect of this war that would shock and horrify the world: the systematic killing of six million Jewish people by the Nazi regime.

The breadth of this genocide—the wiping out of an entire group of people—was unparalleled in history.

After World War II, the Soviet Union and the United States faced off as the two most powerful countries in the world. Thus began the Cold War, a state of political and economic tensions between these two nations, inflamed at times by propaganda and covert activities. It brought a new anxiety to the world as the two vied for power, backed up by weapons that could destroy the world. Finally, in 1990, after many political shifts and changes, the Cold War ended, and relations between these countries became more friendly.

Despite the vastness of these conflicts, they were not the only ones in the twentieth century. Wars, dictatorships, and struggles for independence affected much of Africa, the Middle East, parts of Asia including Korea and Viet Nam, and Eastern Europe. All the conflicts changed political boundaries, altered governments, made some people poor and others rich, affected people's values, and left some feeling helpless, some flippant, some fearful.

Wars bring about social change, as do advances in technology. There was plenty of both in this century. Just a sampling of the ingenuity of twentieth-century technology would include television, helicopters, air conditioning, movies, skyscrapers, the use of insulin, microwave ovens, common use of automobiles, iron lungs and a polio vaccine, tape recorders, x-rays, heart and other organ transplants, space exploration, fertility drugs, video cam recorders, computers, and the Internet.

Along with technological changes were psychological advances. The work of Freud, Jung, Adler, Kohlberg, and many others had a profound effect on how people viewed themselves, family life, mental health, and society in general.

In the western world, women gained status slowly. In 1919, after fifty years of struggle, American women won the right to vote. Women over age thirty won this right in England the year before. Other attitudes about women's roles in work, government, families, and religion shifted over the decades. The kinds of work available to women changed with the needs of their countries as well as through the efforts of activists. Education for girls varied greatly from country to country throughout the world.

Many "just for fun" items and events developed, part of what would be called "popular culture." Some would have a lasting effect on society; others were enjoyed and then forgotten. A few of these phenomena are: Mickey Mouse, dance marathons, the Orson Welles radio broadcast which frightened many Americans, the jitterbug, Bugs Bunny, Smokey the Bear, the bikini, McDonald's restaurants, rock music, hula hoops, Elvis, the Beatles, Barbie dolls, pop art, flower children, skateboards, roller blades, video games, and tee-shirts with slogans.

In the twentieth century, the Catholic Church grew as never before, the majority of Catholics living in Asia, Africa, and South America. In the first half of the century, the Church faced the horrors of war and the challenges of Fascism and Communism. Many Catholics suffered martyrdom while working to save their Jewish brothers and sisters during World War II. Numerous Catholics kept their faith alive under repressive Communist regimes.

As the century progressed, so did the Church, under the leadership of the warm, intelligent, and humorous Pope John XXIII.

He called for an ecumenical council, mainly to promote the unity of all Christians and to study how the Catholic Church could adapt itself to the rapidly changing world. The Second Vatican Council, or Vatican II, brought renewal, questions, new direction, fears, and change. It began in 1962 and closed in 1965, but is still the underlying guide for the Catholic Church as it enters the twenty-first century.

Human rights violations were rampant in this century; heroes and heroines emerge from times such as these. Anne Frank spoke for the persecuted, and Eleanor Roosevelt spoke for the oppressed. Martin Luther King worked for racial equality while little Ruby Bridges bravely and prayerfully faced the hatred of adults in order to begin building that equality. Mahatma Gandhi, Bishop Dom Helder Camara, Archbishop Oscar Romero, Dorothy Day, Marie Curie, Nellie Bly, Mother Teresa, Albert Schweitzer, Albert Einstein, Jackie Robinson, Rosa Parks, and Evita Peron, as well as hundreds of missionaries who died in Singapore and the Philippines under Japanese rule, all contributed to efforts of peace, freedom, and the dignity of all of God's people. They are the heroes and heroines of the twentieth century.

Edith Stein was one of these heroic people. In the first century, Saint Paul was a Jewish Christian; in Edith Stein we have come full circle to the story of another Jewish Christian who spread Christianity and died for her faith. Edith was killed in a concentration camp in 1942. Pope John Paul II beatified her as a confessor and martyr in 1987, and in October of 1998, Edith Stein was canonized. Her feast day is August 9.

The Story of Edith Stein

Edith Stein was Jewish by birth, Christian by choice. She was a great seeker of truth, and her story is interspersed here with Scripture passages that reflect her search. Have one reader tell the story, then lead children in a choral recitation of the Scripture passages.

Before beginning the story, explain to children about the Jewish Day of Atonement, Yom Kippur. On this day, Jewish people fast from all food and liquids, to atone or to make amends to God for evil and sin.

It was the Jewish day of Atonement, Yom Kippur, in 1891. A baby girl was born to the Steins, a Jewish family in Germany. Her family never imagined how her life would one day be given in atonement for the evils of the world.

Little Edith was very quick to learn, and determined to be independent. Soon she was working hard at school, and was especially good at reading and writing. However, because she was Jewish, her prejudiced teachers never admitted she was the top student in her class. Edith questioned many things she learned, even her Jewish religion, which her family was carefully teaching her. By the time she was thirteen, Edith knew she was looking for truth. She read books, she talked with people. And then she decided that there was no God.

Chorus   But they do not come back to Yahweh their God or seek him (Hos 7:10).

Edith kept studying, and later entered Goettingen University to study philosophy as part of her search for truth. The famous and brilliant teacher, Edmund Husserl, taught her. Edith worked hard, but she also enjoyed hiking trips and lunch in little cafes. She spent long hours talking with her many friends, discussing new ideas, searching for truth. Professor Husserl was so impressed by Edith's work, he invited her to be his assistant. Many of the teachers were Christians, and soon Edith's quick mind was learning about their beliefs. She had many questions, but no answers.

Chorus   Send out your light and your truth; they shall be my guide (Ps 43:3).

Then, a war broke out. It would be the worst war the world had ever seen, and Edith's country was in the middle of it. She volunteered in a hospital, working as hard there as she did in her classes. She was well-liked by the wounded soldiers. When the war ended, Edith was able to return to school and earn another degree. She became Doctor Stein when she was only twenty-three years old. Her country was hurting from the war, and Edith worked politically to help. Still, she searched for truth, and now she wondered whether the teachings of Jesus might give her some answers.

Chorus   All who are on the side of truth, listen to my voice (Jn 18:37).

One night, Edith stayed at a friend's house. Before going to sleep, she chose a book from a nearby shelf. It was the autobiography of Saint Teresa of Avila. Edith read all night. At dawn she finished, and knew her truth: she would be baptized in the Catholic Church.

Chorus   I am the Way; I am Truth and Life (Jn 14:6).

Soon Doctor Stein was teaching at a Catholic women's college and becoming a famous writer. She wrote about Catholic philosophers like Saint Thomas Aquinas, and she wrote and spoke about women's role in religion. And, she wrote about Christ's choosing to atone for our sins by dying on the cross. Even as she was seeking truth, she was teaching it.

Chorus   Let your minds be filled with everything that is true, everything that is honorable, everything that is upright and pure (Phil 4:8).

Another great war was brewing. A man named Adolf Hitler ruled Germany, and he had a hatred for Jewish people. He formed an evil plan: he wanted to kill all the Jews in his country and those in other countries, too. He started by not allowing Jewish people to hold certain jobs. Despite her conversion to Catholicism, Edith was considered Jewish and could no longer teach at the college. About this same time she decided to join the Carmelite Sisters, and to continue her writing there. Long before many other people did, Edith understood that Jewish people were in greater and greater danger every day. She believed that her Jewish and Christian background gave her a special way of serving God. She prayed, telling Jesus she was willing to give her life in atonement for the great evil in the world.

Chorus   I came into the world for this, to bear witness to the truth (Jn 18:37).

Edith was moved to a convent in Holland where the sisters thought she would be safer. But soon, Hitler's soldiers, the Nazis, were persecuting Jews in Holland. The Catholic bishops protested, and this made the Nazis furious. Now anyone who had been Jewish and became Catholic was in danger, too. Edith was soon arrested and taken to a concentration camp, where many people were made to suffer and die. Edith was not afraid, even though she knew that she, too, would soon die. She spent her time in that horrible place praying, and caring for children and their mothers, all of whom were terrified. Then, on August 9, 1942, Edith Stein was martyred in the concentration camp.

Chorus   You will come to know the truth, and the truth will set you free (Jn 8:32).

Activities

1. Edith Stein spent her life searching for truth. Look over the saint stories from previous centuries. Discuss who else might be seen as searching for truth.

2. Since the twentieth century is the one your students were born in, discuss with them the major events of this time, and look for signs of Christ's light in these events. Children can make a book of these signs, using magazine pictures, newspaper stories, or drawings they create. Interspersed on the pages can be Scripture quotes about Christ as our light, such as John 1:9, 8:12, 9:5, and 12:46.

3. Today's children inherit a multicultural religion. Encourage them to research Catholic traditions in a variety of cultures. An example would be learning how Spanish-speaking American Catholics celebrate the feast of Our Lady of Guadalupe.

4. Encourage children to learn of another twentieth-century martyr, Maximilian Kolbe. One good resource is *Maximilian Kolbe: Saint of Auschwitz* by Elaine Murray Stone.

Timeline

Using the information at the beginning of this chapter and in the story, finish your timeline by adding the twentieth-century segment.

More Saints (and Saintly People) of This Century

Katherine Drexel (1858-1955); John XXIII (1881-1963); Bertilla Buscardin (1888-1922); Maria Goretti (1890-1902); Miguel Pro (1891-1927); Maximilian Kolbe (1894-1941); Catherine de Hueck Doherty (1896-1985); Dorothy Day (1897-1980); Caryll Houselander (1901-1954); Mother Teresa (1910-1997); Archbishop Oscar Romero (1917-1980); Maura Clark (1931-1980); Thea Bowman (1937-1990); Dorothy Kazel (1939-1980); Ita Ford (1940-1980); Jean Donovan (1953-1980).

Suggested Resources

Bausch, William J. *Pilgrim Church* (Mystic, CT: Twenty-Third Publications, 1998).

Beers, Burton F. *World History: Patterns of Civilization* (Englewood Cliffs, NJ: Prentice Hall, 1991).

Bunson, Margaret and Matthew. *Lives of the Saints You Should Know*, Vol. 1 & 2 (Huntington, IN: Our Sunday Visitor, 1994).

Dues, Greg. *Catholic Customs and Traditions* (Mystic, CT: Twenty-Third Publications, 1994).

Ellsberg, Robert. *All Saints* (New York: Crossroad Publishing Company, 1997).

Foley, Leonard, OFM, ed. *Saint of the Day* (Cincinnati: St. Anthony Messenger Press, 1990).

Hynes, Mary Ellen. *Companion to the Calendar* (Chicago: Liturgy Training Production, 1993).

Jockle, Clemens. *Encyclopedia of Saints* (London: Alpine Fine Arts Collection Ltd., 1995).

Kramer, Ann, and Lindy Newton, ed. *Quest for the Past* (Pleasantville, NY: The Reader's Digest Association, Inc. 1984).

Lovasik, Rev. Lawrence, G., S.V.D. *Best-Loved Saints* (New York: Catholic Book Publishing Co., 1984).

Oliver, Jane, ed. *The Warwick Atlas of World History* (New York: Warwick Press, 1988).

Palisin, Victoria. *Saints: A Lively, Loving People*, Vol. 1 & 2 (Villa Maria, PA: Center for Learning, 1993).

Savary, Louis M., STD; illustrated by Sheilah Beckett. *The Children's Book of Saints* (New York: Regina Press, 1986).

Sisters of Notre Dame of Chardon, OH. *Saints and Feast Days* (Chicago: Loyola University Press, 1985).

Stevens, Clifford. *The One-Year Book of Saints* (Huntington, IN: Our Sunday Visitor, 1989).

Walsh, Michael. *Book of Saints* (Mystic, CT: Twenty-Third Publications, 1995).

Whalen, Michael. *Seasons and Feasts of the Church Year* (Mahwah, NJ: Paulist Press, 1993).

Of Related Interest...

Praying With the Saints
30 Classroom Services for Children
Gwen Costello

You and your students (grades 3 to 6) will enjoy using these 30 creative prayer services and activities, each of which focuses on an aspect of a saint's life that children can imitate. Each service includes a brief introduction, a mini-biography of the saint, ideas for prayer, an action response, and an optional activity. An ideal resource for every religion class, a must-have for every classroom library.

104 pp, $12.95 (order J-30)

Saints for Children
Stories, Activities, Prayer Services
Mary Kathleen Glavich, SND

Features 12 popular saints and emphasizes virtues and how middle graders can practice them in their lives. For each saint there is a lively account of his or her life and good works, a prayer service, discussion questions, a craft, activities, and a puzzle or game.

80 pp, $9.95 (order B-40)

Saints for Our Time
Ed Ransom

Presents each saint as a real person, with similar problems, hopes, fears, and dreams as the reader. There are saints for every person and personality, each with a different set of qualities, talents, weaknesses, and attributes. Written in response to the needs of catechumens and RCIA candidates, this volume is recommended reading for every catechist, teacher, student.

304 pp, $14.95 (order B-38)

Book of Saints
Michael Walsh

Here is a saint for each week of the year, some well-known, and some who deserve to be better known. Each saint's biography opens with an illuminated capital that depicts a scene or notable quality identified with that saint. These saints can serve to renew our own commitment to faith, prayer, and loving service.

160 pp, $9.95 (order M-20)

Saints Alive
Stories and Activities for Young Children
Gayle Schreiber

Here is a delightful book of short stories illustrating the lives of 30 saints for children in grades pre-K through two. Each story focuses on a positive aspect of the saint's life, offers a prayer to that saint, and includes an activity page.

72 pp, $9.95 (order M-68)

Available at religious bookstores or from:

TWENTY-THIRD PUBLICATIONS

P.O. BOX 180 • 185 WILLOW ST. • MYSTIC, CT 06355 • 1-860-536-2611 • 1-800-321-0411 • FAX 1-800-572-0788

Call for a free catalog